I DON'T WANT *to* TAKE CARE *of* MY MOTHER

How to Forgive the Woman
Who Neglected YOU!

EVE ROSENBERG

© 2020 by Eve Rosenberg

All rights reserved. No part of this book may be reproduced in whole or part, or stored in a retrieval system, with the exception of brief quotations embodied in critical articles or reviews, or transmitted in any form or by any means, electronic, mechanical, photocopying, recording, or otherwise, without the written permission of the author. Requests for permission should be addressed in writing to author at Eve@lessonslearnedinlove.com.

ISBN: 978-1-7328506-4-4
Library of Congress Control Number: 2020904017

Printed in Delray Beach, Florida, USA by Eve Rosenberg

DISCLAIMER

This book is designed to provide general educational information about the subjects discussed and not to diagnose, treat, cure, or prevent any psychological, or emotional condition. It isn't intended as a substitute for any diagnosis or treatment recommended by the reader's psychiatrist, psychologist, or any other medical practitioner. Use of this book does not establish any doctor-patient relationship between the reader and the author or publisher.

The author does not assume and hereby disclaims any liability to any party for any loss, damage, or disruption caused by errors or omissions, whether such errors or omissions result from accident, negligence, or any other cause. No warranties or guarantees are expressed or implied by their choice of content for this volume, and there is no guarantee that these materials are suitable for the reader's particular purpose or situation. If you suspect you have a psychological, or emotional problem, we urge you to seek help from the appropriate specialist. This book isn't intended to be a substitute for the advice of a licensed physician or mental health provider.

Readers must rely on their own judgment about their circumstances and take full responsibility for all actions and decisions made because of reading this book and applying the recommended practices.

The author has made every effort to ensure the accuracy of the information within this book was correct at the time of publication. Any perceived slights of specific persons, peoples, or organizations are unintended. All names have been changed, and any reference to a specific story or instance is coincidental.

For more information, visit www.lessonslearnedinlove.com or www.peoplepleasersreformacademy.com

*To my late parents, Livia and Leslie Rosenberg.
I share my truth with the best of intentions.
May the soul of our family be healed.*

FOR JUDY

Keep forgiving Mom

ACKNOWLEDGMENTS

Many supporters of mine, both indirect and direct, made invaluable contributions to the creation of this book.

First, to my mother, Livia Rosenberg. I'm dancing with you every day. I feel you all around me and I can't get enough of your essence. I miss you terribly.

To my father, Leslie Rosenberg. I see you happy and free and that brings me peace. Thank you for all that you've taught me, the good and the bad. I love you and live in honor of you.

To my sister, Judy Legare, who was with me in the womb and stood beside me throughout our childhood. This book is for us.

A special thanks to Arlene Fleischman, aka the redhead, for being a constant source of confidence in my life and a very dear friend. I love you!

To my dear friend, Vivian Vertes, who encouraged me to stick with this subject matter when I was sitting on the fence about whether or not to move forward. I am blessed to have you in my life.

Thank you to the late Debbie Ford, my teacher, my mentor, the woman who gave me my life back. Your brilliance continues to teach me to live fully.

A special thanks to Elisa Pike, Lois Vacianna, Tanisha Blythe, and Amarel Wilson-Peets, for taking such wonderful care of my mother. I am forever grateful.

Thank you to the wonderful staff at Stratford Court Assisted Living for supporting my mother in so many ways. She was incredibly happy there.

So much gratitude to my writing coach, Sam Horn, The Intrigue Expert. You're brilliant and have brought out the writer in me. Because of you, there will be more books to come. There are no words to describe my thanks to you.

Huge thanks to my life coach, Mindy Schrager. You're invaluable to my existence in everything I do. I'm grateful for all your support.

A huge thanks to my publishing coach, Diana M. Needham. Your support has been amazing and without you this book wouldn't be published. And thanks for helping to put out fires, too!

Many thanks to my proofreader/editor, Phyllis Amaral, for making this book clean and ready for the world!

Thanks to Lisbeth Tanz for helping out with editing.

A million kisses for my dogs, Tabitha and Priscilla. You gave up your playtime to sit by my side as long as it took to get this book finished. To Meadow and Ashley across Rainbow Bridge. I miss you. My fur babies inspire me to love, and it makes my life precious.

TABLE OF CONTENTS

A Note to the Reader xi
Introduction xxi
Chapter 1:   Revealing Your Truth 1
Chapter 2:   Priorities First 11
Chapter 3:   Bad Mothers 21
Chapter 4:   It Takes Two 29
Chapter 5:   Understanding Her Journey 39
Chapter 6:   Revealing Your Story 49
Chapter 7:   The Purpose of Forgiveness 63
Chapter 8:   Reopening Your Eyes 89
Chapter 9:   Think Before You Act 97
Chapter 10: Power Plays Aren't Powerful 103
Chapter 11: The Biggest Lie I Ever Told 109
Chapter 12: Putting Down the Baton 117
Chapter 13: Last Chapter, Last Day 123
Epilogue 133
Notes 137
Additional Resources 139
About the Author 141

A NOTE TO THE READER

For years, I envied people who were blessed with a mother who nurtured them in a positive way; who protected them and defended them at all costs, and who, I imagined, would run in front of a train to save her children.

"If only I had a different mother," was the mantra I chanted for years. I wished for the mother I needed and struggled with the one I had, fantasizing about where I'd be in my life *today* if the *right* mother had been bestowed upon me.

I can only assume that if you're reading this, you and I have something in common. We didn't win the "Great Mother Lottery." I can further speculate that you desire to feel differently. Otherwise, you wouldn't be holding this book.

But before you get the impression that I'm about to bash my late mother or play the victimized daughter, let me set you straight. My intention is to be brutally honest and share my truth. Some of it isn't pretty. Overall, this book qualifies as a love story and a "how-to guide" to support forgiveness with the most important woman in your life: Your mother. Once you do, you'll be well on your way to nurturing the most important person in your life: *You*.

Whether your mother is alive or deceased, forgiving her is essential to living your best life. It's not imperative that she remain in your life, that you engage with her, or that you even like or love her. If the relationship is toxic, keeping your distance is a wise choice. But to live a happy life, you must understand where your journey began and find your way to accepting and forgiving her.

Your mother's steps have preceded yours, and whether you know it or not, believe in it or not, or like it or not, the circumstances and trauma she's faced in her life, the choices she's made for her life, live on in *your* DNA. Even if you've chosen a different path and strive to be nothing like her, your mother's journey is every bit a part of yours, both physically, emotionally, and even spiritually. There's more than meets the eye, and it concerns more than just the experiences you've had with her. The life she's lived way before you were born affects you, not just in the person she's become and her ability to be a mother, but also unconsciously within your emotional connection to her through DNA.

Have you ever felt depressed and scratching your head as to why? Nothing happened to cause the doldrums, but even so, you're feeling so low that you don't want to get out of bed. Aside from a chemical imbalance, an emotional disorder, or an obvious stressor in your life, your depression may be a result of how you experience the wounding of your predecessors.

Each of us belongs to a Family Soul, and we're affected by the generations that came before us. It's no accident that people who are adopted somehow sense and yearn to know where they came from. The adage, "blood is thicker than water," has more credence than we may suspect. It's a connection we can't escape from. Just as our mother's journey is a part of ours, the steps we take now and continue to walk after she's passed on are part of the Family Soul. If we desire to heal, we're not the only ones who will benefit. Our efforts have the potential to heal the predecessors that lived before us. We can heal our Family Soul. This is great news, because it means that we can make a difference not only in our lives but the lives of our past family members as well as the future generations to come. For more information on Family Constellations and the Family Soul, search the internet for books written by Bert Hellinger. I mention it here merely to make a point. Forgiveness and healing have a massive impact. What a gift!

For much of my life, I've struggled with the concept of forgiveness. As a young child, I carried deep anger. I knew something wasn't right with my family and it confused me. Because I was discouraged to express myself, my feelings made themselves known through eye infections and migraines. As I grew older, I became ashamed of my dark feelings and worked hard to cover them up. I became pleasant and nice. Before long, I'd become an avid People Pleaser. But deep down, I was suffering.

After my second divorce and a bout of panic attacks in my mid-forties, I sought to heal my struggle and discovered my spiritual path. It was comforting to learn there was an unseen force bigger than me to support me. I prayed to find my way. With the teachings I immersed myself in, I learned that forgiveness isn't about letting people off the hook or justifying their offenses or abuse. Instead, forgiveness is a way to break free from the hold others have on us that keep us from moving forward and living a joyful life. This news was exciting to me, because I was angry with many people, including my mother. I put forth a lot of effort into changing my feelings, but nothing was working. Each time, my resentment grew. This new perspective was helpful, but even so, I found my willingness to let go turning into an uphill battle. I realized that my expectations were in the way. I believed that by forgiving someone, it meant wiping the slate clean and continuing a relationship with my offender no matter what. This backfired in big ways, because it prevented me from setting boundaries and implementing consequences with the people who betrayed me and who remained in my life. And, where all evidence indicated I should run for my life, I found it difficult to walk away from certain people, which kept me in toxic relationships way too long. This whittled away at my self-confidence and had me holding on so tightly, I left claw marks behind.

In my search to find middle ground where I could forgive others while honoring my anger and true feelings, I discovered a way that honors my anger and disappointment while allowing me to let go and move on. I'll reveal how I apply forgiveness in my life and how it works like a charm in a later chapter. There's much to say before taking that final step. I'm certain you'll find it interesting enough to want to try it in your life. It helps to make the process of forgiveness not only possible but probable. And its effects are long-lasting. Stay tuned.

If you're not attracted to the benefits of forgiving your mother just yet, perhaps knowing that doing so will have a direct impact on the relationships you attract *into your* life, may be a good motivator. I'm a firm believer that we seek resolution with our family of origin in every relationship we engage in. For the wounding that happens early on in our lives, we seek to make sense of who we are, why we're here and what we're meant to do. Above all, we need to know we matter and that our lives have meaning. Resolving our hurt from childhood takes precedence toward healing.

When you better understand your mother's journey, you'll better understand your own. And in doing so, you'll leave a meaningful legacy behind. Living your best life will fill you up in ways you can't imagine while honoring your mother as well, despite her misfortunes and the neglect and abuse she inflicted upon you. In the end, we must return to love, at least if only in our hearts. This can only happen once you've forgiven your mother and yourself. Real joy only happens with a heart that's filled with love.

If you examine the challenges you've already faced, your relationship track record, and the abusive relationship you've built with yourself, you'll understand that your self-image was affected by your relationship with your mother. This isn't a theory I can prove to you, and it isn't even my theory. It's an established fact that your mother is an important role model in your life and that she's a big part of your early conditioning. My intent is to support you in revealing that in all your relationships. You're seeking resolution for your struggle that happened early in life and to make sense of why things happened the way they did. By turning the pages of this book and giving my recommended practices a fair shot, my intention is to encourage you to recognize that your mother's journey has valuable wisdom for your future. Making peace around your past will change your life in positive ways in the present and ensure that the future looks bright. Clarity comes by making sense of things.

In the pages to come, I'll share step by step, how I changed my relationship with my mother both in my interaction with her as well as deeply within the recesses of my psyche where my victim story thrived for years. Inside this tale, forgiveness was forbidden, and life was unfair. For decades, I struggled with dark beliefs about myself and where I came from. "I don't belong," became a theme in my story and it affected every aspect of my life. It took countless jobs and three broken marriages to realize I didn't feel at home anywhere. Even years of therapy didn't reveal the depth to which I suffered by holding onto the resentment I felt for my mother. In fact, therapy encouraged it.

But once I forgave my mother, new and exciting opportunities came my way. Before long, I was able to fit in wherever I chose, provided I desired to be there and understood that not everyone sees things the same way I do. Either way, I must recognize that my opinions are important, and my voice is valuable. Once I connected that I was present for all the experiences in my life and that being the common denominator in all my relationships gave me the power to change my life and make it extraordinary, I learned that I was looking in all the wrong places for answers. This realization began my journey of going inward for information and cleaning up the areas of my life that were causing me pain. Because I didn't feel worthy, deserving, capable and entitled to a great life because of who I believed I was and the shame of where I came from, the self-image I carried of myself was very grim. And, because I blamed my mother for everything, it's not surprising I was dragging around some very heavy weight. All of this was keeping my joy at bay and my life at a standstill. The only solution was to forgive and let some light in.

If you're finding it challenging to forgive your mother, it may be because you haven't yet acknowledged *the dark truth* that you've been hiding from yourself and others; or, you've been minimizing, justifying and rationalizing to avoid dealing with it: *The resentment you hold for the woman who made you feel unwanted, neglected, and wrong or who put you in harm's way by exposing you to a victimizer, playing favorites with your siblings, exploiting you for her personal gain, or being so narcissistic or passively absent that you got cast aside.*

Whatever the abuse or neglect was about, the negative judgment you're holding onto is eating away at *you* and sabotaging *your* chances to be happy. You're the only person who can bring closure to your struggle. It's likely that your mother never will. Stop waiting for things to change; they won't. By not forgiving and accepting your mother, you're attacking and rejecting YOU!

I've grown to believe that we're all wounded in some way. Deep scars surface and linger long past the aftermath of neglect, abuse, and abandonment. Most of us fear rejection and aloneness because we've already experienced a toxic dose. We fail to acknowledge this truth or we either dwell in or minimize it. Finding balance will support closure, correction, and resolution. The victim doesn't transform into the victor without acknowledging that they've been victimized in the first place. We must recognize that we deserved better—and so did our mothers. We all got screwed. In the real world we live in, wounded people grow up and have children. Victims become victimizers. If we've survived our adversity, there's good reason. It's up to each of us to discover why. As Aristotle once said, "Knowing thyself is the beginning of all wisdom."

When we run from our struggles, we latch onto an imaginary lifesaver in hopes of preventing ourselves from drowning in the dark, vast ocean of fear. The problem is that the habits and addictions we use to cope, i.e., eating, drinking, over-working, gambling, shopping, retreating, procrastinating, or other ways that ultimately work against us, are short-lived strategies that don't directly address our problems.

In fact, solutions stay at bay and we continue to deepen our suffering. It's up to us to take radical action if we want to change our circumstances and attract joyful experiences into our lives.

The depths to which I blamed my mother for all my life's drama, exposed itself when I was faced with one of the biggest decisions of my life: to relocate to Florida to care for her in her mid-eighties. My father had died suddenly the previous year while enjoying himself in a hot tub. My mother depended on him for everything. As she increasingly struggled to fend for herself, it became clear to me that she needed help.

In conjunction with my mother's set of challenges, I was making the tough decision to leave my unhappy marriage. I had a few ducks of my own that needed lining up if I wanted to create a promising future for myself. I was living in the Northeast, which made it difficult to be attentive to my mother's care. I was looking for a loophole to shimmy my way out of this obligation and felt the most reasonable excuse *should* suffice. *My whole life is in New York; I can't leave. Everything I know and built is here.* And yet, the nagging voice inside me drowned out the chorus of how and why I shouldn't go. *What kind of person wouldn't be there for her own mother?*

Still grasping for an escape plan, I argued that my sister and her husband were now settling in Florida. Perhaps they could manage my mother's primary care while I visited from time to time. I could take a seat on the bench and ride out the game. But as quickly as this idea hit home, guilt won out and tossed me back in the playing field and up to the batter's box. Relieving myself of responsibility had a downside. I had my own shame and anger to live with. I didn't want to move to Florida, and I didn't want to take care of my mother. *Not one bit.* I didn't like hot weather, and I wasn't happy about being so close to my mother's cold demeanor. My mind wouldn't rest. *She didn't take care of me! Why should I take care of her?*

Anxiety circled me like a school of sharks. My impending divorce was taking a contentious turn, and a future in Florida was a scary prospect. Back then, I not only believed I was making a bad choice in moving near my mother; even worse, it would lead to my demise. *Am I trading one nightmare for another?*

Despite my trepidation, I set out on my journey a few months later on a sweltering day in July. I traveled with my furry companions: my Yorkie, Meadow, and my Brussels Griffon, Tabitha. I'm forever grateful to my loving cousin, Vivian, who insisted on accompanying us so I wouldn't be alone. We wore special t-shirts she'd had printed. As we left my home for the last time, I wasn't privy to my soon to be ex-husband's reaction as he read the back of our shirts: "And for this reason, I'm out!" This was a phrase made famous on the TV show, Shark Tank. Essentially, it means *No Deal!*

I planned the trip meticulously to cover four days of driving. We'd spend four and a half hours each day on the road and spend the night in a dog-friendly hotel that AAA had reserved for us. We were only an hour and a half into our journey when a bad migraine set in. I had to pull over. Just as I was losing faith that we'd catch a break, I spotted a motel off the exit that accepted dogs. Our arrival date in Florida was now in jeopardy, and our unscheduled stop meant we had to rebook all our hotel reservations. It was a temporary frustration for I learned later that, had we stayed on schedule, we would have driven straight into a hurricane on our third day. I realized I just needed to trust and have faith that things would work out. I would be fine.

Fast forward five years. This realization proved to be true.

I couldn't have imagined the joy and sadness that awaited me as I made that trip. Just shy of five years from the day I arrived in Florida, I lost the woman I was overjoyed to finally find and bond with. The cherry on the cake was that I not only forgave my mother; I fell deeply in love with her.

As I remember my mother, I thank her, bless her and live in honor of her as I soak up every ounce of joy I can get my hands on. She's with me everywhere, and I know she's cheering me on. I'm rooting for her, too, and hoping that she's profoundly happy wherever she is. She had so little joy in her time here on earth. It wasn't until our final years together that I could understand, appreciate, and sympathize with her journey.

I often wonder where life would have carried me had I made a different choice. I'm certain I'd have cheated myself out of the extraordinary joy and peace I experience today if I hadn't forgiven my mother. Finding compassion and forgiveness for my mother allowed my heart to open wide to accept and love myself. And as a result, I'm attracting special people into my life and experiencing meaningful relationships that bring me deep connection and joy. I can say with conviction that I'm free of resentment and happy at last.

No matter how angry, sad, or hopeless you may feel right now, there's renewal whenever you're ready to claim it. As *A Course in Miracles* so beautifully states: *"Forgiveness is the Key to Happiness."* I reap the rewards every day, and you can, too. All it takes is curiosity, willingness, and the desire for a better life.

Every relationship needs a hero. If you're willing to rise to the occasion, you're the one who will benefit the most. I invite you to read on. It's time to claim your right to inner peace and happiness.

You deserve it.

INTRODUCTION

How did I end up here? my mind screamed.

Fear had befriended the anxiety I was feeling for days. I was working diligently to quiet my thoughts, but another would quickly chime in. *What if I can't handle this?*

Arriving in Florida after a long journey south, rendered me tired and hopeless. I dreaded the future. It took every ounce of strength I had to summon up mere scraps of positivity—knowing that what I think about, I bring about. The chatter in my mind needed some serious tweaking. It was my first day out to meet my mother.

The clock struck noon and the air was balmy. The weather forecast threatened high heat and thunderstorms by late afternoon. Here I was in the sunshine state, blindly feeling my way through the dark. The semblance of a life that once promised happiness was now a blur in my rearview mirror. It was bittersweet saying goodbye to my life in the Northeast.

As my eyes scanned the bare, beige walls of my new apartment, I remembered how I'd rented it sight unseen. When I visited the property a couple of months ago, most apartments were tenant occupied and unavailable for viewing. All I had to go by was a small floor plan inside a brochure. I wasn't privy to the lack of natural light past ten in the morning or the walls that screamed out for a paint job. This place wasn't exactly a perk for the melancholy mood that occupied my mind.

It had been three days since I moved in and I was barely acclimated to my new surroundings. I slept on an air mattress and lived out of a suitcase. My midsection was beginning to show the diet of takeout meals I was forced to eat because the movers—and my pots and pans—weren't expected for another week.

It felt strange being on my own in a new state. Even though I wasn't a stranger to Florida, I was on vacation there frequently. It wasn't a place I ever thought I'd choose to call home. There's a transient energy with people coming and going. Those who eventually settle here escape the frigid temperatures elsewhere, while the natives resent the intrusion of the snowbirds who arrive in late October, creating traffic snarls on the roadways and crowds in stores and restaurants.

Nuzzling close to my dogs was the only comfort I could count on. They were my saviors, preventing me from falling into a deep well of sheer loneliness. I had no idea how long I'd stay here. What was clear was that I needed to take care of myself, now that I was faced with the burden of taking care of my mother.

I tip my hat to families who graciously support each other through every phase of life and seem to be at peace with it. Parents care for their grandchildren while their children are working, and when they reach their elder years, the obligation rests on the shoulders of the younger generation. Case closed.

My maternal grandmother, Adele, lived with us until her sudden death when I was twelve. She was like a mother to me and my sister. She looked after us even when my parents were home. It gave my mother the luxury of napping during the day and leisure time for my father when he returned home from a long day's work, usually well after we were tucked in for the night. Even so, the house was quite small, which didn't allow for privacy. I suspect this arrangement had a negative impact on my parents' already strained marriage, evident in the lack of affection between them.

When I was in my forties, I imagined my parents or in-laws, once they reached an age where living alone was no longer safe, would live with me and my husband. When I turned fifty, and my parents were settling into their early eighties, my fear steadily grew. My present-day reality echoed that tomorrow wasn't far off. As my father would often say, "It's not a matter of *if;* it's a matter of *when.*"

As my clients and friends shared their experiences with me, my concerns increased to a volume I could no longer ignore. Those who chose to move in with a parent became disillusioned and very unhappy. They revealed incidents where their parent became combative, abusive, and extremely difficult to care for. They begrudgingly admitted that their own patience had also waned, producing reactive outbursts toward their ailing parent. If this didn't tip the scales in favor of running the other way, most admitted their marriage had taken a harsh blow because of this arrangement.

Here I was, facing the proverbial midlife crisis people talk about when they've lost sight of life's direction. Standing squarely at a crossroads, experiencing a life-altering change at the age of fifty-five was not my idea of a happy place to be.

Ending my third marriage and realizing that my life had taken a U-turn from the direction I'd predicted when I married for the first time at twenty-five, was more than I could handle. Back then, I believed my children would be grown by the time I reached fifty years old. My husband and I, free from childrearing, could travel and do what we chose. I was thrown for a loop when that marriage came to a screeching halt after only eleven years. When my faith in love got me to the altar two more times, those unions had an even shorter distance to the finish line, and none of these unions produced the children I'd always wanted. For all the time, sweat, and tears I put forth in relationships, I came out with a minus return on investment. Becoming a caretaker to my mother wasn't something I embraced. Resistance was becoming my constant companion. This was just another monkey wrench thrown into an unpredictable mix of misfortune.

Since I didn't want to take care of my mother but felt obligated to take charge, she became my number one obsession. Even before her dementia kicked in, my mother wasn't easy to be around for more than half an hour. Meeting her for lunch today was my first challenge. One hurdle at a time.

The darkly lit restaurant set the tone for the somber mood I invited. The hostess led us to a booth in the back room. I took a seat across from my mother. The knowledge that I now lived close by and had agreed to take charge of her care stifled my breath. I couldn't stop coughing.

During lunch, my mind drifted to when my father was alive, and I'd make short trips to visit. I'd be eager and excited to see my parents, as if miraculously we'd all make a radical shift and morph into a Norman Rockwell painting. Every trip, this hope was squelched as quickly as it came. I was met with the sarcastic, flippant comments my father made. My mother wasn't interested in talking with me. Instead, she focused on pushing food in my mouth. Inevitably, dark thoughts filled my mind, persuading me that my parents didn't love or care about me. Predictably, these trips ended on a bleak note. Afterwards, I was left with an enormous amount of anger at myself for using my much-needed vacation time from work to travel to see them. Each trip ended badly and left me reeling for days. My salvation during those visits was knowing that I'd be heading home within a day or two. Now, looking squarely at my mother across the table, I was home. *Nowhere to run. Nowhere to hide. Help!*

There are resources. I assured myself. *Dad was meticulous, obsessively preparing for the future, always putting his ducks in a row. Mom was left well off financially after his sudden death. Thanks, Dad!* Even though my mother was scared and believed she had no money, there was a healthy nest egg to see her through. It drove me crazy to have to remind her of this each time fear got the best of her. But when the insurance company confirmed that she had only twenty-five thousand dollars of aide assistance after she canceled her fifty-two-year policy due to a rate increase, my fear rose up to meet hers. *How long would the money last once she needed round-the-clock care? People live much longer these days. She's only eighty-six. She can live to one hundred!*

Then there was God. *God only gives you that which you can handle.* God knew I couldn't handle living with my mother, so he blessed me with options. My mother was settled in her apartment and I lived twenty-five minutes away in mine. At one point, my sister insisted my mother move in with her and her husband, but my mother, still in her right mind, adamantly declined. She was unwilling to be a burden on her daughters. That was one thing we happily agreed on.

Just in case you're wondering what would have become of my mother if there was no money, my sister lived out of state, and I had been faced with what to do, I would have invited her to live with me. I don't consider myself to be a cruel person and couldn't imagine anyone out on the street homeless, much less my own mother. I would, however, have prayed with all my might that the roof would cave in on both of us and end my misery.

It didn't make me feel good to dislike my mother. Deep down, I yearned to *want* to be there for her, to care for her, and to cling to each moment we had left together. I even remember thinking before my dad's passing that taking care of my mother would be my opportunity to bond with her. She was under his control and this blocked our ability to develop our relationship into anything good. But even with my father out of the picture, all the years of stifled resentment for how my mother wasn't there for me got in the way of my desire to give our relationship the fresh start it deserved.

As lunch was winding down, we shared an apple cobbler and drank some tea. I was anxious and tongue-tied. As I looked straight into my mother's eyes, and before I could make sense of what I was going to say, an avalanche of words came tumbling out.

"Mom, I want to help, but you need to understand I have a life too. I can't be chauffeuring you around all the time." My tone wasn't pleasant, and I don't know what I expected her to say. *Was I hoping she'd talk me out of it?*

Even though my mother needed support, she wasn't demanding and never once suggested that I or my sister move near her. I don't think she thought things through. She resisted facing her future alone as an elderly widow and at the same time was childlike and fearful. All the evidence suggested she wasn't taking sound measures to care for herself. With guilt being a big motivator and obligation its twin brother, I took it upon myself to take on the responsibility. And I didn't lose the opportunity to blame my mother for my decision. As the tears in my mother's eyes became visible, so did the glaring stare from the woman at the booth beside us. *Please floor, swallow me up so I can free my evil self. Spare me and my mother the humiliation.*

Coming off like a *bitchy, selfish, horrible daughter* who doesn't want to help her mother out, I reverted to what I know best. I beat myself up. I profusely apologized and set out to convince my mother that I wanted to be there for her. When I got home, I reached out for every emotional coping skill I'd mastered to get me through the night. I ate everything I could find in the refrigerator, binge-watched Dateline, and fell asleep with the TV on.

The following morning, I abruptly awoke as if an intruder had broken into my home and startled me out of a deep sleep. My body formed into a perfect forty-five degree angle on a flimsy air mattress, a challenge even for the avid athlete, which hardly describes me. For a moment, I couldn't make sense of my surroundings and my heart was pounding. As the room grew familiar, I felt a warm blanket of comfort suddenly embrace me. To my surprise, the intruder who woke me just moments ago was, instead, a savior in disguise, delivering the assurance I needed to know that I would be okay. I listened intently to the whisper coming deep from within my being that vied for my attention.

"Give yourself permission to dislike your mother," the voice said. "Stop resisting and honor your feelings. Your heart will open." Even though this message initially confused me, I made a commitment to follow its direction. In hindsight, it proved to be the first step toward easing my struggle in my relationship with my mother. Accepting my negative feelings about her would soon open doors I couldn't have imagined at the time.

As an emotional wellness coach who supports others in healing, I make it my business to walk my talk. "Listen to your intuition," I often tell my clients. "Trust your gut and follow it." Here was my opportunity to take my own encouragement and let things unfold.

Things began unraveling as quickly as a ball of yarn falling down a tall flight of stairs. I had embarked on an inner journey that would lead me somewhere truly remarkable. Now, only a few years later, I've retraced my steps since arriving in Florida and developed a sound process with specific practices that has supported me in forgiving my mother and healing my relationship with her.

Celebrating what I refer to as a personal victory, I began writing this book about my journey. As you read, this process will reveal itself. If you're willing to give my recommended practices a shot, you, too, can experience the gift of forgiveness with your mother. This book is my gift to you in hopes that you find peace and resolution in your life.

There's no greater joy than making sense of where we come from. And this "making sense" is crucial if we want to accept and love who we are. Forgiving your mother will open doors to opportunities that have been patiently waiting to meet you.

"Knock. Knock."

"Who's there?"

"Whoever you want it to be. Open the door and you shall see."

Chapter 1

REVEALING YOUR TRUTH

You can lie to yourself, but the truth will keep knocking.
It's time to open the door.

"I don't think you understand. I've disliked my mother for years!" I watched as Lana's eyebrows slowly crept up her forehead, forcing her eyes to open wide.

It was another hot, sunny day in Florida. Seated at a table in the breezeway of a popular restaurant in Delray Beach, we were surrounded by specialty boutiques crowded with busy shoppers browsing the sales. We were in a prime location for people watching. Being an avid dog lover, I chose this venue to watch canine friends as well. I commended the establishment for accommodating clientele with their fur babies in tow. Large aluminum bowls filled to the brim with water and biscuits sat on the floor beside the hostess station. A quick glimpse inside revealed small and large breeds alike, some curled up, their heads resting on sandaled feet, others sitting patiently in hopes of scoring a treat. All the while, their masters were busily chatting and dining on scrumptious salads and French bistro fare.

"We all have issues with our Mothers, but we don't really hate them." Lana interjected.

Lana and I met in kindergarten. Our families lived nearby on a quiet street in Westchester County, New York. Parents felt safe to let their children play outside on the grassy lawns and ride bicycles on the streets, so long as they stayed close by and minded the infrequent traffic. We kids were on high alert for one four-wheeled vehicle that showed up right on schedule each day.

One of my fondest memories was playing outside on a beautiful day as the sun beat down on the open street. With the beads of sweat forming on my forehead, I'd take off the sweater my mother insisted I wear and then kick off my shoes. I loved seeing how long my bare feet could tolerate the scorching concrete before I'd scream and run for cover on the grass. Suddenly, my ears would perk up as I heard the faint melodic chimes announcing the arrival of the ice cream truck. As it slowly turned the corner, a giggle burst from my small frame, which exposed my excitement to the others. They joined with me in collective laughter. We all made a mad dash to be first in line.

My mouth watered seeing the white truck covered with colorful depictions of the cold treats inside. My favorite treat was the devil's fudge pop. It was made with vanilla ice cream and chocolate fudge covered in a lumpy, chocolate powdered coating all hiding a chocolate candy center. My mother gave me enough money to buy two pops; one for me and one for my sister, Judy. Tearing off the paper wrapper, I took care to not break the candy center as I gently bit into the pop, savoring each bite. I'd focus on nothing else but the pleasure of the cold treat as it melted in my mouth. It put me into a trance every time.

In the years that followed, Lana and I remained friends. We hosted slumber parties at our respective homes with a few other girls. We joined the Brownies and walked door to door selling cookies. As we grew older, movie outings and shopping excursions took precedence. We came to know each other's families very well over the years. When we graduated from junior high school, my parents broke the news that we were moving to another town in a different school district. This news was a huge blow to us both. We vowed to visit often, but soon life got busy. Our visits were replaced by phone calls and, over time, those stopped, too. We gradually lost touch. Years later, we were thrilled to reconnect on Facebook.

Lana was in town from New York to visit her elderly parents, giving us the perfect opportunity to meet up for lunch. I spotted Lana when I arrived early to secure our reservation. I had to pinch myself to remember how much time had passed. "You look exactly the same!" I yelled out. I was beaming. We hugged and then ordered a couple of lattes and salads. We chatted excitedly, exchanging the lowdown on husbands, exes, families, and careers. With those topics out of the way, Lana finally asked a flurry of questions: "Why did you move to Florida? Was it to take care of your mother? Are you happy?" Her questions had barely landed before I started talking.

"Yes, I moved to be close to my mother. But no, I'm not happy about it, and I don't want to take care of her. I'm struggling." I considered Lana an excellent person to share with since she was so familiar with my backstory. She listened intently, although I saw her flinch more than once as I talked. I saw a glimpse of sympathy in her eyes. She too, didn't have an easy relationship with her mother. I had to wonder whether I was stirring up some pent-up resentment she didn't want to deal with.

"One day, I got so angry at how passive my mother was being, I had a super scary vision come to me," I said. "I imagined waving my hand in front of my mother's face. 'Is anyone home?' I asked her. All she did was give me a blank stare and say her usual response, 'What did I do?' I was so angry that I grabbed the handle of one of those super heavy Le Creuset pots and hit her over the head with it in hopes that she'd wake up! For days, I was horrified I could even think such a thought."

As I heard myself talking, I realized I wasn't taking care to censor myself. My unedited rant revealed my deepest, darkest feelings. And those feelings were gaining momentum. By the time I stopped to take a breath, there wasn't a doubt in my mind that Lana knew the extent of how deeply I resented my mother and how I blamed her for the disappointments in my life. "If only I had a different mother, what I could have become."

Even though I didn't feel good judging my mother in such a negative light, my anger was overriding my shame. It's as if I had been holding my breath all these years. My resentment had become a toxic sludge of pent-up rage. Pushing away my dark thoughts only fueled the fire of resentment toward my mother, which was counterproductive to healing my relationship with her. Saying my truth out loud allowed me to breathe deeply again. I felt that a heavy burden had been lifted as if I'd released a long-held secret that I couldn't bear to hold on to another minute. *Does this explain why I feel so nauseous and sick in my mother's presence? Is this why she can't do anything right in my eyes?* I was beginning to wonder how much of a part I played in our disconnection.

The conversation at lunch with Lana sparked a new beginning for me. I made a promise to myself that I wouldn't hide from my truth, as ugly as it was. And in the days that followed, I received more insights that showed I was going about everything in ways that damaged my relationship with my mother instead of helping it. And, what I was doing was having a very negative impact on my life, my relationship with myself, and my connections with everyone else.

As cathartic as it felt talking to Lana, I discovered that my need to share had more to do with seeking validation and sympathy from her. I was full of self-doubt, since I made myself wrong for how I felt. It's easier to find others to agree with us than to admit that our perspective makes us a bad person. Over time, I've learned that whatever we feel is real to us, period! I realized that I'd been searching my whole life for people who could convince me that I was lovable. But deep down, I felt angry and mean. I didn't know it back then, but I see it clearly now. Because I felt like a bad person, and I didn't trust myself. People who agreed with me by blaming others, created the sense that I was in fact, the good guy. It never occurred to me that my poor self-image created and attracted those negative experiences. And, because I wasn't guided or educated to think any differently, the toxicity kept growing.

It wasn't until I learned that a power greater than me guides and protects me, all the answers I seek are within me, and the power to change my life and relationships is my choice, that I understood it was me and the judgment I carried that needed tweaking. I needed to turn away from those who supported my old worldview and face the mirror. It felt good to blame others, because it was the only way I got to be right about anything—and *being right* meant having value.

I stopped beating myself up and claimed my right to have all my feelings. Suddenly, I felt right all the time. Not right in that everyone else was wrong, but right based on *my* perspective. Other people had their perspectives, too. It wasn't that any of our perspectives were wrong, it was just that we have different ideas about things—our versions of reality.

Armed with this new understanding, I contemplated some of my feelings about my mother. *I don't like my mother! I'm angry that she neglected me! I'm angry she didn't protect me, and I blame her for all that's wrong in my life! It's all her fault. She didn't take care of me, so why should I take care of her? I feel like a horrible person feeling this way, and, if I'm honest, I hate myself even more than I hate her.* When I finished, I could see that I was living my life deeply entrenched within a victim story and that my self-image needed a radical makeover.

As I examined my relationship with my mother, it now made sense that being defensive and combative when I was with her was my way of letting her know she hurt me. It was my way of seeking the apology I needed from her that I was confident would never come. It seemed unlikely that my mother would take responsibility for her behavior because she couldn't or wouldn't see it. Trying to get her to change was my strategy for getting her to love me. But when all my attempts failed over time, I was left feeling disappointed, angry, and defeated. I believed I got cheated out of the mother I needed and deserved: a woman who would love me, teach me, and guide me to navigate life as a winner. Instead, I got a weak, helpless, detached, tuned out, passive woman who chose to live a miserable life with a man who abused her and who didn't lose an opportunity to send the message to her children that "They'd never amount to anything good." *My truth!*

One benefit of revealing such a deeply buried secret to yourself, and even better to someone you trust such as a therapist or coach, is that all shame loses its power and hold over you in time. Eventually, it no longer affects your life or impacts your choices. The solutions, options, and possibilities you didn't notice before, because you were too focused on what wasn't working or how you'd be exposed in some way, are now available to you.

Even though I felt like a bad daughter and was ashamed of speaking my truth, it was liberating when I did. The shame, resentment, and humiliation I felt about myself around the feelings I had about my mother prevented me from experiencing real joy in my life because I believed all of it made me unlovable. Plus, hiding my feelings took an enormous amount of energy. All of my relationships were strained, including the most important relationship, the one I had with myself.

The resentment I held for my mother was a double-edged sword. Whenever I entertained negative feelings about her, I was also attacking and rejecting myself. Because she was my mother, the woman who birthed me, my place of origin, I was directly part of her journey. What I had yet to learn was that her life trauma changed who she was as a person long before I was born. I wasn't privy to this insight in the past, nor did I understand that my thoughts and emotions were affected by her life experiences as well as my own thoughts and experiences. Trauma has lingering effects that pass from generation to generation through our DNA. I was beginning to wake up to the truth that as long as I rejected my mother, I wouldn't feel as if I belonged anywhere. Not accepting my mother meant not accepting myself. It's no wonder I felt so lost, untethered, and afraid in much of my past. The moment I became aware of this pattern, I was able to implement change. The awareness and acknowledgment of what was really going on opened my eyes to hope and faith. My healing journey had begun.

My lunch with Lana was the spark that began a transformation in my relationship with myself and my mother, even though I didn't know it at that moment. As time went on, I felt entitled and validated to have all my feelings. And to my surprise, I realized it wasn't my mother's acceptance that I'd yearned for all these years; it was my own. This epiphany opened the door for my curiosity and desire to learn more about my mother and her life, a woman who I judged harshly and who was a mystery to me. I wanted to understand why she couldn't be there for me in the way that I needed her to be. And I also knew the answers wouldn't come from her. It was up to me to imagine what I could with the information that I had and to explore further about earlier times in her life. I wanted to know where my journey began, and I wanted to understand and forgive my mother.

A big part of this process was to allow things to unfold naturally. It required that I be radically honest with my feelings and be kind and compassionate to myself. I needed to recognize that I deserved good things, including having a great mother. I also needed to remember that my dreams were important, and that I was entitled to have them. This helped me regain my hope of becoming a great daughter too, a role that I could be proud of. I yearned for the desire to *want* to care for my mother instead of feeling obligated to support her. I wanted to seize the opportunity to experience the honor and privilege that some people have described as they lovingly support someone in their last stage of life. I hoped to be left with fond memories instead of pent-up resentment. And, I yearned to live out the rest of my life feeling worthy and proud to be *me,* as well as the daughter of the woman who birthed me. *If I live a life that's extraordinarily happy, I can honor my mother's life as well.*

STEP ONE: GET REAL ABOUT HOW YOU FEEL.

Since you can't change anything you don't acknowledge, it's crucial to *get real about how you feel.* If you're angry with your mother, find it difficult to be around her, hold resentment toward her, or judge her harshly, being real about it will facilitate the necessary steps toward forgiveness. I believe it's risky talking to others. My conversation with Lana happened after much reflection and I'm trained as an emotional wellness coach and have had a good deal of support. My greatest encouragement is to seek out a trusted professional so you can sort out your feelings. Many people aren't sure of how they feel, and it's common to keep our truth hidden even from ourselves. A professional will help you to understand your feelings whereas a friend or relative may harshly judge you, disagree with you, or make you feel worse.

In the comfort and safety of your own space, be radically honest with yourself and expose the negative judgments you're holding toward your mother. Don't deceive yourself. It's time to cut through the B.S. and get to the nitty gritty of all your feelings, especially the darkest ones. Consider it a detoxification. Don't judge yourself and understand that *all* feelings, even the ones that surprise you and have you questioning your integrity are human. We all possess both light and dark qualities, so find comfort in knowing that *we're all everything.* Whatever you become aware of and acknowledge will be released to make room for change to occur. Anything you deny will remain and fester. What you think about you bring about, so get excited to learn more about the way you think. To fill your mind with positivity, don't push away the negativity; acknowledge it and give it its merit. I suggest keeping this information in a journal. If you're afraid it will be discovered, write it and then destroy it. The exercise will be just as effective. Writing things has a way of making them real.

Next, make a list of all the things your mother did and didn't do that left you feeling neglected, abused, or unloved. This is your opportunity to uncover the resentment you're holding on to so that you can process it and let it go. You do this not to forget, but to forgive. Just like you can't change what you don't acknowledge, you can't forgive what you don't acknowledge. Even your darkest feelings can support you in ways you can't imagine. They're part of your emotional intuition and will help to protect you, keep you from danger, and support you in making good choices. I encourage you to approach this exercise with willingness, kindness, and compassion. You're not crazy to feel like a victim; you were victimized. But the victim doesn't become the victor without acknowledging the victimization. People who minimize their feelings are hiding them and denying them to not feel pain. You must be radically honest about your feelings if you want to discover the patterns that keep you from having the life that you want. When you acknowledge your feelings, you'll be able to implement positive change in your life. If you hide from them, nothing will change.

Breathe and acknowledge yourself for taking this first courageous step on your behalf. It's the most loving thing you can do for yourself and for your mother. Connecting with your feelings, particularly your anger is the way out of your pain. Exposing your victim story in full will help you make peace with it. Life is all about the meaning we give it, so the wisdom you find will help you reach a place of clarity about who you are, why you're here, and what you're meant to do. It's the deeper meaning that helps us to know that we matter and that we're worthy beyond measure, that adds joy to our lives. In turn, this helps us to become more loving to ourselves and others, which contributes to the betterment of the world.

The first step is most often the hardest and most courageous. After that, walking down this path will become easier. Later, you'll feel joyful enough to skip down this path. You can stop here and do this exercise or continue reading to learn all the steps before you begin. Whichever way you choose, know that you're on your way and I salute you.

Chapter 2

PRIORITIES FIRST!

Better hurry and choose you before you lose you for good.

"I choose me!"

I said it with conviction and in front of the mirror. It was a long time coming. At last, I understood what I had to do next.

Now that I had given myself permission to dislike my mother without judging myself as an evil person, my next step was to find a practical way to handle her needs while making myself my first priority. It was time to take charge of *my* life. To create a happy experience for myself, while still being a support for my mother, I had to manage my time schedule wisely. Sacrificing my needs and desires was no longer an option. That's what made me disgruntled in the first place. Every time I had the thought of having to do something for my mother, it felt as if I was taking something away from me. *If it weren't for her, I could this or do that—*

I remember hearing the news of my father's death. He had died suddenly, and it was a shock. Initially, I broke down and cried. I loved my father very much despite anything that happened between us. But after I wiped away the tears, I was surprised to hear a strong voice within me say something that felt liberating. *Now you're free to live your life.* I was a grown woman approaching my mid-fifties, but still affected and controlled by my father and what he thought about me. The small relief that somehow comforted me into believing I was free to make my own choices was overshadowed by the deep conditioning of *better live the should life*. Even when what we think is an obstacle, once it's removed, we often remain stuck anyway.

I understand that a primary cause for my resentment toward my mother was I made her responsible for my own neglect. Since I blamed her for not being a good role model, I allowed her lack of guidance to diminish my ability to learn sound ways of taking care of myself. *If my mother didn't take good care of me, then I don't know how to take care of me.* If I looked to my mother for guidance and didn't get it, I got angry and beat myself up over it. *No one's taking care of me, so I won't either!* It was time to grow up, take responsibility, and own up to my sabotage. Otherwise, my life would never become my own and it wouldn't be joyful. It was time to stop People Pleasing and doing what others wanted me to do. It was time to stop abandoning myself.

Since my list of resentments against my mother was long, I didn't need any more animosity filling my head. I had to be diligent in my commitment to myself, declaring to me, my mother, and the Universe that from this day forward, I would choose me first. This meant swallowing my concerns about appearing selfish and self-absorbed, two qualities I previously frowned upon and thought I didn't possess. As an avid People Pleaser, I believed the misguidance that helping others first is the noble path in life. I didn't think I was being self-serving, because I left myself out or at best, put myself last. Boy was I in for a big surprise!

I was now certain that to have the life I wanted I had to understand that being *selfish and self-absorbed* wasn't bad. It was the *only* way for me to move forward. To take care of myself, and to fully desire to support others, this understanding was a necessary step on my journey. I developed a mantra to help in this understanding. It had a threefold purpose: to lift my spirits, to remind me of my new way of being, and to help sink in that I deserved a happy life. I obsessively chanted this mantra:

"I choose me first!"

I committed to filling my days with work, leisure, and fun. I allotted the time I needed to attend to my mother while getting all my needs met before hers. I included a daily morning and evening ritual where I prayed to God for a positive outcome. I didn't want to hold on to the guilt and resentment anymore, and I wanted to feel in control of my own choices while making myself my first priority. My deep hope was that I'd achieve this *and* that my feelings toward my mother would radically change. *Please God, if you grant me one wish, grant me this: I want to feel love for my mother and summon the desire to support her without losing myself.*

I clung to the hope that one day I'd want to love and care for my mother without feeling obligated, guilty, and left without a life of my own. I yearned to be the daughter who deeply bonded with the woman who birthed her and to savor every moment she had with her mother while she was still here in the physical world. A believer in miracles, I imagined myself forgiving my mother, connecting deeply with her, and creating a bond where we would live in harmony and enjoy each other's company. It was a stretch, but it was also a positive goal to strive for.

So, on a particularly challenging day out with my mother, I got creative. As I felt my patience waning while she was her usual negative, judgmental self, I challenged myself to suck it up. When we stopped at a store that my mother wanted to browse in, I suggested she go inside while I wait in the car. While she was gone, I closed my eyes and pretended that she was no longer alive. I imagined that she'd passed some time ago, and I missed her deeply. I spoke to God silently. *God, I miss my mother. She's been gone a while now, and I would love to have just one day with her to remember and cherish. Let this be the day you bring her back to me.*

When I opened my eyes, my mother was knocking on the passenger window for me to open the door. "I didn't like anything in there," she said. I looked into her eyes and was astonished at how calm I felt. There wasn't anything I needed to say to make her feel better or disagree with her. I was actually happy to see her. "You look so pretty," I said. And remarkably, her mood shifted too. She threw me a wide smile, and we drove away as if we'd made up for everything in the past. I continued to compliment her. "I love your sweater. I love being with you. I missed you while you were in the store." It became a very pleasant day. I felt a sense of gratitude for our time together as if it were fleeting; and of course, it was.

Believing that someone will always be in our lives is something many of us take for granted. This day was a victory for our relationship. My mother's demeanor followed mine and quietly we celebrated a shift in our connection. We didn't speak about it. It was a quiet understanding. As we said goodbye that day, I smiled the whole way home knowing that I had far more control than I ever thought possible and that it was time to take responsibility for contributing to the toxicity of our relationship. It wasn't my mother's fault alone. This revelation brought me much joy because I was letting go of my victim story a little bit at a time.

Even though that day was special and revealing, our relationship didn't continue without its challenges. During the next several weeks, I sensed that my mother wasn't doing well living by herself. She was cooking less, had old food in her refrigerator, was becoming forgetful about medication, and began repeating herself. I suggested we see a doctor and have someone stay with her for several hours a few days a week. She complied with the doctor's visit but was quite resistant with the idea of allowing a stranger into her home.

At first, I didn't force anything and allowed her to call the shots. I also believed I was losing her, and that thought terrified me. I was afraid of what lay ahead, and I believed there was no way I could handle it nor did I want to find out if I could. Since I'm being truthful, there were times I wished she'd die in her sleep, so I could be spared what I knew was coming.

Eventually, I had to take charge because I felt she was in imminent danger. It's as if a fire was lit underneath me. I acted quickly and began looking for options. I could see that I was cowering to her objections and demands and not wanting to make waves or upset her. I was allowing her to determine what she needed when she wasn't in her right mind. It felt eerily similar to the way she parented me. There was no guidance, discipline, or encouragement. And that's when I had a light bulb moment. It was time to remove my daughter hat and become her parent instead. To further motivate myself, I imagined that I was competing with my mother in a *Who's the Better Parent?* contest. I committed to becoming *a better parent* for her than she was for me. I had faith I'd win. Soon, I possessed the elixir that would lead me to success.

I moved quickly to implement the plan I knew needed to be in place. I became the prime decision maker for my mother's care. I obtained a legal power of attorney while she was still able to understand and sign documents. It was a responsible move on my part. If I hadn't done this, once her dementia worsened, I wouldn't have had as much authority when it came to her care or her finances to support it. It also cut through a lot of red tape and made the process move along more easily. I had a plan for what would happen after she passed, even though no one knew when that time would come.

As my mother needed more time and attention, I revised her care plan, including bringing in the strange women who came to live with her. In time, she stopped resisting so much and surrendered to being pampered. This made my life much easier, too. I had plenty of time to run my business and enjoy my personal life with friends while still carving out time to spend with her. Unless there was an emergency, I visited her three days a week and I stuck to that schedule. I also made it a practice to phone her every night to ask her about her day and to speak to her aide. Managing our lives in this way helped me feel fulfilled in my life, and it increased my desire to see my mother and spend quality time with her.

My family was blessed that my father left my mother financially stable, but either way, there are options to consider. I hear many people say they would never put their parents in a home to later make that choice once their marriage has been threatened. It's not abandoning a parent if you do not have the means to take care of them in your home or if it means your life is sacrificed. These arrangements can have negative consequences for everyone involved. I know many people who can vouch for this truth.

My sister wanted my mother to live with her and her husband. When I discussed this with my mother early on, she was adamant she didn't want that. And, I don't think my sister stopped to think how her life would have been affected. "I don't care," she would say. "She's my mother. You don't abandon your mother." That left me thinking. *Why is it we are so willing to abandon ourselves no matter what?*

I firmly believe that it is more damaging to everyone involved, to abandon the self by taking on such an enormous responsibility, particularly not being trained as a professional to extend the proper care to a person with special needs. And if we bring in the *selfish* conversation, I believe that being selfish is necessary and loving, if we want to live authentically in our connections with others, as we all say we do. Searching for the right place to house a loved one is more loving than bringing them home and abusing them when all patience and tolerance has no more room for any kindness or compassion. This happens way too often.

By putting myself first, I was able to prioritize my needs and my mother's needs. The result was two happy people getting the care and attention they both needed and deserved.

STEP TWO: CHOOSE YOU FIRST.

Whether you're involved in your mother's life or not, it's important to *choose you first*! If you're People Pleasing or leaving yourself out of your life in some way, you're bound to resent many people along the way, especially the people you're already keeping a resentment list for. It's common to find "Mom" or "Dad" at the top of the list with the heading: "Who do you blame for the condition of your life?"

Taking charge of your needs and desires makes it possible to see new perspectives. Once you're filled up and satisfied, you don't have to rely on others to rescue you or take care of you, which was probably an illusion at best.

This is a good time to put a plan into place. To forgive others and yourself, you need to implement strategies, so that you live in integrity with your feelings and values. It's important to recognize and honor yourself in terms of what's acceptable for you and what isn't. It's time to consider: What are your deal breakers? Where do you need to set boundaries? What are the consequences for your offenders?

If you don't have a strategy in place, you'll be wishy-washy with your choices, break promises to yourself, and give up on your commitments. You'll live a life without integrity. Once this happens, a domino effect of self-sabotage ensues that further erodes your efforts.

Begin by saying these words out loud, if you choose, when you're alone and silently when with others: "I choose me!" "I'm my first priority!" These helpful mantras remind you of your intention, especially when someone is asking you for something and you feel uneasy saying no. They will help shift your priorities into place. Remember: *You* come first!

I find it helpful to look in the mirror and tell myself that I love and approve of myself no matter how much I or others may be judging me. It's a big support to write the mantra, "I choose me. From this day forward, I matter most!" several times a day in your journal. Chant these words during your workout or in the shower. Keep reminding yourself of your new priority.

Warning: For those of you who believe this is a selfish and self-absorbed practice, be aware that there's no avoiding being these qualities. If you are a human being with an ego, you're an automatic member of the *Selfish, Self-absorbed Club.* For those who believe this isn't the way to be in this world, give yourself some sound time to reconsider that there's an agenda behind everything we do. Even people who see themselves as *selfless,* perhaps by donating monies anonymously, do so for the feeling it brings them. Giving "anonymously" brings the feeling of generosity without condition, which can bring joy to the *giver,* coupled with a feeling of superiority for not wanting anything in return. There's always a motive behind what we do. And, even when we turn away others' generosity by not allowing ourselves to receive, that's selfish too. We're not allowing others the joy of giving. We can't avoid it, so stop trying. We're all selfish, period! The sooner we stop avoiding it, dancing around it, and making selfish a dirty word, we'll prevail. And in that process, we'll become kinder and more compassionate with everyone. It's a win-win!

Whether you're People Pleasing, making sure everyone else comes before you, or giving all your monies to charity and believing you're a selfless individual, let me assure you that we *always* give to get. And, in my strong opinion, I believe that it's not possible to authentically forgive the people whom we deem more important than ourselves, because, to move on from the offenses of others, we must have our backs first. Self-care and self-love are necessary to become objective and compassionate with others. Otherwise, we're glossing over everything and just mouthing the words.

Helping others is an honor and a privilege and doing it brings immense joy to everyone. All the ways we set out to experience joy is for the self. The selfish expression I believe most people frown upon is the narcissistic expression of "Others don't count. I'll take everything for myself and leave nothing for you." This isn't what I am suggesting at all. A person who's truly filled up with love for themselves becomes a natural giver and spreads love wherever they go.

Once you swallow the myth that "selfish is bad," and you get busy with your self-serving choices, you'll find that doing for others becomes a desire instead of an obligation. The one thing we've had right all along is that serving is truly joyous. What kills this opportunity every time is the myth that sacrificing yourself for others is the path toward a full and happy life. Instead, it's the path toward resentment and illness. The greatest cost is that it's a dead end to attaining love.

In your relationship with your mother, you must choose yourself first. Keep it your secret if you wish, but you must do it. You'll see your confidence and the desire to share more with others increase quickly. We want to be the best we can be as people, and we want to connect with others deeply and joyfully. The action of serving yourself first will bring about the opportunity to serve others in ways that will pleasantly surprise you.

Chapter 3

BAD MOTHERS

Neglect isn't just in the eyes of the beholder;
it's recognized by law.

Dr. Phil often says, "A mother's job is to protect her child, to guide them to discover who they are, and to teach them how to take care of themselves in the world." My sentiments exactly! So, why aren't many mothers doing just that?

What constitutes a bad mother? As my beautiful grandmother, Adele used to say, "You can look up and you can look down." Let's look way down for a moment, since this book isn't about good parenting.

One of the well-known *bad* mothers that comes to mind is Joan Crawford, Hollywood's movie star of the Golden Age. Christina, one of Crawford's adopted daughters, told of her abusive ways in the book *Mommie Dearest*, named after the loving salutation Joan insisted her children use. In the movie, Faye Dunaway played Joan Crawford, a narcissistic woman who mentally and emotionally abuses her children. Entering her children's room around 3:00 a.m., she goes into Christina's closet, where she discovers an expensive party dress hung on a wire hanger like the kind dry cleaners use. Her eyes bulge out of her head as she begins screaming, waking up her children. They bear witness as Crawford spirals into a ballistic rage, throwing things about the room and covering the bathroom floor with cleaning detergent.

She then insists Christina, who is horrified and apologetic, clean it up at once. The abusive language she uses to demoralize her children, "rotten, spoiled and bad," is impossible to overlook.

Then there's Dee Dee Blanchard, a woman who convinced her healthy, young daughter Gypsy that she was ill with all sorts of illnesses including leukemia, epilepsy, muscular dystrophy, asthma, and other serious ailments. It wasn't until Dee Dee was murdered by Gypsy's boyfriend that investigators realized Dee Dee suffered from Munchausen by proxy syndrome. By then, Gypsy had been subjected to years of uncomfortable medical procedures, countless medications, unnecessary surgeries, and wheelchair confinement despite being able to walk. Dee Dee forced her daughter to fake her illnesses to friends, neighbors, and the media. Having a sick daughter meant Dee Dee could be seen as "the good mother" as well as take advantage of kindhearted people and charities. Around 2012, Gypsy met a man online who became her boyfriend. Together, they planned the murder of her mother. One night in June 2015, he stabbed Dee Dee to death while she slept. Gypsy hid in the bathroom. The pair fled to Wisconsin where they were caught. Both stood trial; Gypsy for murder in the second degree and the boyfriend for murder in the first degree. Both were convicted. The story is so hard to believe. Dee Dee Blanchard would be on the top of my list of *The Worst Mothers Ever*.

As a young girl, Gypsy suffered the consequences of the life her mother chose for her. She endured needless medications and surgeries. Yet, until she was older, there was no indication she had anything but affection for her mother. A newspaper story I read as a teenager has this familiar storyline. A four-year-old boy was rushed to the hospital after being set on fire *by his mother*. He suffered from severe burns on most of his small body and didn't survive despite doctors' efforts. Incredibly, even though she was the one who'd hurt him, he screamed for his mommy to help him. If this doesn't prove how deeply a child loves and depends on even an abusive parent, I don't know what does. Heartbreaking!

Stories of abuse and neglect told to me by clients offer similar made-for-movie horrors. These include stories of:

- Being locked in a closet as part of a disciplinary strategy to quiet down a child's hyperactivity. The child's screams were ignored for hours at a time.
- Sexual abuse by a father and a mother who knew but did nothing to stop it.
- Waiting at school for a mother who never came. The mother disappeared and was declared dead. She reappeared one year later.

Then, there are the many horrible things bad mothers say to their children. "You are evil!" "I should have had an abortion when I got pregnant with you." "You're so different; we didn't know quite what to make of you." "The world would be better off if you weren't in it."

There's no shortage of abusive behavior and, unfortunately, no shortage of bad mothers. As children, we fall prey to all kinds of toxicity from these bad mothers. What's even sadder is that victims, without proper intervention, often grow up to be victimizers.

If you're a mother yourself, you might be wondering how you stack up given your history. I understand that question because I know I wouldn't have been a stellar mother when I was younger. Maybe today I'd be a better mother, but I've gone through years of emotional healing to reach this point. Honestly, I'm glad I didn't perpetuate the behaviors I was raised with. Given what I know now, I'd feel awful if I'd created a child who questioned his or her value and worth in the world like I did.

My mother was a saint compared to the bad mothers described above. But I've "looked way down" as Grandma used to say, not to compare her to them, but to show the extremes of abuse. The point is this: abuse is abuse. It's that simple. You don't have to be locked in a closet, confined to a wheelchair, or set on fire to experience neglect and abuse. Here's a portion of an article by Wikipedia that I found online defining child neglect. It states the following:

"**Child neglect** is a form of child abuse,[1] and is a deficit in meeting a child's basic needs, including the failure to provide adequate supervision, health care, clothing, or housing, as well as other physical, emotional, social, educational, and safety needs. All societies have established that there are necessary behaviors a caregiver must provide in order for a child to develop physically, socially, and emotionally. Causes of neglect may result from several parenting problems including mental disorders, unplanned pregnancy, substance abuse, unemployment, overemployment, domestic violence, and, in special cases, poverty.

Child neglect depends on how a child and society perceives the parents' behavior; it isn't how parents believe they are behaving toward their child.[2] Parental failure to provide for a child, when options are available, is different from failure to provide when options are not available. Poverty and lack of resources are often contributing factors and can prevent parents from meeting their children's needs when they otherwise would. The circumstances and intentionality must be examined before defining behavior as neglectful.

Child neglect is the most frequent form of child abuse, with children born to young mothers at a substantial risk for neglect."

The reality is that neglect and abuse come in many forms. What's important is how *you* were affected by your childhood. We're not aiming to play the blame game or rate your mother on a "Bad Mother Scale," but we will hold her responsible and accountable, because she should be. For the sake of healing and moving toward forgiveness for your mother, I don't suggest you concentrate on pointing the finger without understanding what made your mother the way she is or was. We will discuss this in another chapter. What's important is whether *you* felt neglected and abused as a child and whether *you* may still feel this way in your relationship with your mother. Your feelings matter most, and if you're feeling them, they're real. One of the biggest struggles in life is living with self-doubt. That can drive anyone crazy and make for a life of struggle and uncertainty.

When I talk about my mother, I often say, "She wasn't a bad mother, she just wasn't a mother." When I coined that phrase, I was plugged in emotionally to my victimhood. But today, I understand it more clearly that my mother was a fragile woman who never healed from the traumas inflicted in her youth. She couldn't effectively take care of her own needs much less mother her children.

If you were an outsider looking in on my family, you'd probably say what many of my friends said, "I love your mother! She's so nice!" My mother was sweet, innocent, childlike, and friendly. It's easy for others to experience your parents differently than you do, since they don't rely on them for nurturing and guidance. As I got older, I found it particularly annoying when my friends would praise my mother because I felt it negated me and my feelings. I needed to be validated, which meant I needed other people to dislike my mother to justify my feelings.

Emotionally detached and unavailable parents can do the same, and sometimes more, damage than physically abusive parents can. People who grow up emotionally neglected typically have a poor self-image, using sabotage as their currency to get attention. Others suffer from debilitating depression, causing them to emotionally withdraw and living their lives by going through the motions.

As emotionally passive and unavailable as my mother was she did do motherly things, such as driving us to ballet class, telling us to practice our piano lessons, preparing dinner, and packing our trunks for camp. But when it came to nurturing, guiding, comforting, or encouraging her children to steer us toward success in life, my mother wasn't *home*. I consider this incredibly abusive. I grew up and became an adult without knowing how to navigate the world, much less believing I was incapable of taking care of myself. It was a most frightening way to live.

People who lack confidence, are maladjusted, and who don't love and care for themselves can hardly do a stellar job of taking care of children. Our misguided thinking that we must *aim to please others first and make them happy* has backfired and produced People Pleasers, serving everyone else except themselves and their families. They don't see the deeper messages they're sending to their children: *everyone else is more important than you or we don't care about you.* Because they're exemplary role models in their communities, it's expected that their children will be grateful and well-behaved. But this isn't how the children feel or behave.

Fran's son, who became addicted to drugs at a very early age, created so much turmoil inside the family that the family eventually fell apart. Fran was a busy mother and community leader. She was a soccer mom, Boy Scout leader, and on one board or another during her son's childhood. She couldn't understand why her son felt unimportant and left out. Today, she feels angry, betrayed, and exhausted. She's still taking care of everyone in her community except herself and has resorted to tough love to deal with her son. She takes no responsibility for the way he turned out and lets him know what a great mother she's been whenever she gets the chance. Even though it's a blessing to serve others in our communities, unless we serve ourselves and our families first, everyone will lose in the end. It isn't that Fran isn't a wonderful person with a huge heart. She just failed to see how making others come first meant she abandoned herself and her family.

My mother was hardly the *community mom,* but she was still an avid People Pleaser. Everything was done for appearance's sake. The house looked presentable, we were dressed well, and dinner was served on time. I hardly remember my parents ever arguing. Their communication was more of a sharp silence. At meals together, even well into my adulthood, we ate in silence. The exception was if my father brought something up to shame someone. Then the meal would become downright uncomfortable. My mother was quiet and accommodating. She never stood up to my father, and it was implied she took his side. A black cloud hovered over the dinner table. I remember leaving many of those meals feeling utterly unsupported and alone in the world. I dreaded mealtime.

Sometimes, my father would show up as a hero when least expected. When my sister and I were approaching our thirteenth birthday, my father noticed that we didn't have much homework from school. We actually did, we just weren't doing it. Our homework wasn't something our mother concerned herself with. Shortly after making this discovery, my father researched new neighborhoods with better schools. I must admit, this decision changed my life for the better and afforded me the opportunity to get a good education. Despite my father's bullying ways, I consider him to be one of the wisest men I've ever known. He was great at strategizing and methodically organizing things, so they'd work efficiently. Had I not feared him so much, I could have learned much from him.

It's important to put self-doubt to bed and consider it time to own what happened in your life. If you were a victim of neglect and abuse (and if you're reading this book you probably were), it's time to own it.

STEP THREE: OWN THAT YOU WERE VICTIMIZED.

To move from victim to victor, which is a worthy goal to move toward if we want to live a happy life, we must first recognize and own our victimization. This isn't a time to compare stories and minimize yours when you talk with someone else who went through hell and back and you didn't. This isn't a victim contest of who got treated the worst. In fact, many people have gone through varying degrees of abuse and sometimes the people with the more subtle circumstances suffer the most. Wounds are wounds, and they produce the limiting beliefs we carry into our adult lives. The familiar, "I'm not good enough; no one supports me; I'm unlovable, or I'll always be a loser," are beliefs that can be generated from even the slightest amount of neglect.

Say out loud and write in your journal that you own and accept that you're a victim. The intention is to move powerfully forward using your victimization for the betterment of your life. I believe that we each have a spark inside of us that's ready for us to claim, once we feel entitled and we see our worth. It doesn't appear when things are going well. Instead, it makes itself known when we're forced to take a stand. That's where the strong jolt of *"No more!"* comes from. Passion comes directly from this place too.

I wrote this book because I'm furious about how most people will never reach their potential because of fear or having had their spirit crushed.

Own it. Feel it. Claim it. Breathe.

Remember to be kind and compassionate with yourself and be responsible for your emotional well-being. It helps to have a professional on your side, so reach out. You don't even have to leave your house these days to get support. I highly recommend it.

Chapter 4

It Takes Two

Resentment is a team effort.

"Speak up. We can't hear you."

Ninety-five of us were sitting in rapt attention at a personal development workshop led by the late Debbie Ford. Debbie was a New York Times bestselling author, workshop leader, producer, founder of The Ford Institute, and what I call *a force for healing.*

"What's your greatest shame?" Debbie asked.

It was the afternoon portion of the first day. We had just returned from lunch. By now, participants felt more comfortable to raise their hands and share. Debbie picked on Helen.

"Stand up Helen. Raise your hand and wait for the microphone. Tell us what you feel so ashamed about." Debbie motioned to a workshop assistant to bring the microphone around to Helen. Our seats were arranged in rows on either side of the main aisle so everyone could see the stage.

Helen was visibly shaking. As she spoke, she held the microphone too far for it to pick up her voice. No one could hear what she was saying.

"Speak up. We can't hear you."

I wondered whether Helen regretted standing up. There was a moment of silence, and we could hear her clearing her throat. She held the microphone up to her mouth this time.

"I hate my daughter."

Helen's free hand immediately covered her face, and we could hear her sobbing.

"How long have you felt this way?" Debbie asked.

"For many years," Helen admitted.

"Does your daughter know you hate her?"

"Of course not!" Helen defended. "I think I treat her very well."

"I'd be interested to find out how your daughter feels. Would you be willing to have a conversation with her and share your feelings?" Debbie's voice inspired hope.

"I don't think I'm ready for that," Helen said and sat back down in her seat.

"Who here today has negative feelings about their children?" Debbie asked. Many hands shot up in the air accompanied by some nervous laughter.

It only took a few moments for Debbie Ford to hold the space in the magical way she did for people who desired healing. The conversation became interactive, and we felt safe to share things we've never told anyone before. We were sent off for the evening with an assignment. Without judgment or beating ourselves up, we were instructed to make a resentment list of all the people we're angry with or have negative feelings toward. Then, we were asked to write down our feelings and to give ourselves permission to have them. As a last step, we were to document our experience in our journal.

We arrived at 8:00 a.m. the next morning. Per Debbie's instructions, we were to remain silent during our meals and on breaks. As chance would have it, I sat next to Helen and noticed she looked rested and peaceful. She even appeared younger than the day before. Since we weren't permitted to speak, I smiled as if to say, "You look great today." She returned a wide smile, and we waited for Debbie to take the stage.

When it came time for sharing with the group, Helen volunteered to speak. Standing confidently, and with pride in her voice, she told

Debbie that she'd found the courage to speak with her daughter the night before.

We all leaned forward to hear what Helen had to say.

"I spoke to my daughter as you suggested. When I told Sharon that I was hurt by the strain in our relationship and that sometimes I'm ashamed to admit it, but that I feel hate for her, I almost fell on the floor hearing her response."

"Wow," Sharon blurted out. "Sometimes I hate you too!"

Helen went on to say that Sharon told her that she was cordial and likable because she didn't want to make waves or hurt her feelings. But that she had begun to avoid getting together and declined most invitations with one excuse or another, admitting she didn't enjoy much of their time together. She was happy to receive some honest communication.

"It's like we released a secret, and we're free at last!" We could hear the relief in Helen's voice. "By the end of the call, we were both laughing. We even have a lunch date set up for when I return." Tears welled up in her eyes. "Thank you," she said. Her face shone with gratitude. "What a breakthrough!"

The room erupted with applause and loud cheers as we all celebrated with Helen.

It's common for the people we resent to judge us, too. We're easily triggered around these folks because there's shared animosity. It's not that the other is saying or doing anything obvious, the judgment we carry can be felt in the energy around us. That's why certain people feel bad to us. They deliver their thoughts and judgments in an energy exchange. But when we're keeping an inventory of what's wrong with *them*, how they're going to disappoint us, or how they won't follow through in some way, we're also sharing some of that animosity with ourselves, too.

I believe that our need to be loved and accepted by others in the absence of loving ourselves, is a scary way to live. Plus, it's hard to embody what you don't know or understand. It's common sense that we won't like everyone we meet. We're not meant to connect with everyone. But when our confidence depends on others liking us and they don't, we turn on ourselves. We become part of our own dysfunction.

As I've examined my relationship track record, I realized that I feel the most validated, free of self-doubt, and assured that my feelings are normal and acceptable when I don't make myself wrong about anything. Instead, I own my responsibility for the creation of a toxic dance when collaborating with others who aren't a proper fit for me. When two wounded people come together, it's only a matter of time before toes are stepped on.

One thing I do know for sure, is that if I'm feeling resentment toward someone, they're feeling the negativity too. And in the energy exchange between us, there's either a mutual desire to reach a place of harmony or there isn't. Often, the most loving thing two people can do for each other is to take responsibility for their own behavior, respect that the other has a different perspective, and move on from each other if harmony isn't the mutual goal.

Helen and her daughter Sharon had a positive exchange and were both equally responsible for owning their feelings. The road ahead may be rocky for them, but at least they can stop pretending. We're human. We have dark feelings. Owning them will serve us. Hiding who we are and what we feel doesn't create a new perspective; hiding gives us evidence that we're good at deceiving others and ourselves. That's how we come to live a lie. In time, we forget how we truly feel and end up acquiescing to others because we're unprepared to fight for ourselves.

In the spring of 2011, I experienced what I call *"the cat got out of the bag"* breakthrough in my relationship with my mother. One year had passed since my father's death, and we were holding a memorial service to honor him. I was living in the Northeast and my mother, sister, and brother-in-law flew in from Florida. The plan was to have my mother stay with me in my small one-bedroom apartment. I would sleep on the couch.

After a bittersweet day filled with memories of my father's life and hosting a luncheon for family and friends, we left Westchester County, New York to drive to Fort Lee, New Jersey. During the drive, my sister said something I didn't appreciate, and a disagreement ensued. My mother took my sister's side and then changed the subject. My mind screamed with frustration and resentment. *My mother has never taken my side about anything. Ever!*

When my mother and I arrived at my home, we changed into our nightwear and sat at the kitchen table each sipping a cup of tea. That's when I confronted my mother.

"Mom, why is it that you never take my side in anything? No matter what happens, whatever's said or done, good or bad, you don't stand up for me?"

Donning her usual *what did I do?* expression, she responded with, "You should know better. You're good with people. You're a life coach."

"What does that have to do with anything that just happened?" I demanded. "And, I'm a woman first. Just because I'm understanding, doesn't mean I don't have feelings or that I don't need support!"

But before I could get all the words out, my mother became visibly uncomfortable. She got up from her chair at the table and started pacing about. She even began rummaging through her purse and crying. I felt confident I knew what she was doing. It's what she always does when confronted with something she doesn't want to deal with. She was searching for her NitroMist spray, commonly used to help or prevent her chest pains. I imagined her dropping to the floor and suffering a heart attack on the spot. She'd get off easy, and I'd spend the rest of my life blaming myself for her death. *Here we go. My mother is going to drop dead before my eyes, and I'll suffer the consequences for the rest of my days.*

Even though this wasn't new behavior for my mother, I couldn't be sure if she was pretending, manipulating me, or actually in distress. I thought about an event that had shocked my sister and me that had happened when we were in our early twenties. We were in my mother's bedroom arguing about something insensitive my mother had said to Judy. It was one of those *hit you right in the gut* comments that would trigger most people just for its sheer inappropriateness and lack of compassion.

Judy was triggered all right, and I was taking her side. We both lashed out at our mother, accusing her of being unsupportive. The next thing I remember, is that my mother started grabbing handfuls of fabric of the nightgown she was wearing, while pacing about the room whining and crying. Suddenly, she ripped her nightgown right off her body and stood before us, naked. Judy and I shot a glance at each other that spoke volumes. *Yes, perhaps she's really nuts.* We proceeded to calm her down, even though we didn't fully understand what had just happened. We had no idea what this outburst meant in terms of ever getting support from her. What we did know, was that our mother wasn't taking responsibility for anything she may have done or not done, when it came to her relationship with us. The afternoon ended with our mother popping two valium and going to bed. My sister and I had no resolution or closure.

Back in my kitchen, I watched horrified as my mother clutched at her chest. I rushed to her and proceeded to calm her down. She finally settled down, but only after I had profusely apologized, asked what I could get for her, rubbed her back, and told her to breathe. Shortly thereafter, we turned in for the night.

Surprisingly, I slept like a baby. I was exhausted and diminished from the day before and had no more energy left. I don't remember if I had any dreams, but I awoke the next morning with a doozy of an insight. I was amazed it hadn't occurred to me before. Some things we ought to notice, simply for their obvious nature, and yet they remain hidden from our view. As the old adage goes, *when the student in ready, the teacher will appear.*

I spent years consumed with resentment for my mother for not taking responsibility for having a hand in her children's emotional sensitivity as we struggled to navigate life. It never occurred to me how she might feel as a woman in a horrible marriage who felt she had no other choice but to stay *because of the children.* And, as much as it scared me to admit it, I believed she was miserable being our mother. It's not easy raising twins, much less needy, sensitive ones. For the first time, I could understand the burdens my mother carried and how resigned she became to a life she didn't want.

I heard the water running in the bathroom. Once I knew she was up and about, I called her to join me on the couch in the living room. As she settled in beside me, I put my hand over hers.

"Good morning," I said, looking deeply into her eyes. I felt as if I was about to reassure a child that there's no need to be scared. "Mom, I am so sorry about last night. I regret our argument. I didn't understand it before, but I'm clear now. And I want you to know that I forgive you and that I can only imagine what it must be like for you. If I stayed in a miserable marriage for years because I felt trapped with children, I know I would resent them too."

I think she was surprised. She quickly looked away from me and put her head down. Then, she looked at me with a mix of confusion and embarrassment much like a child would do after being caught in a lie. I suspected her mind was spinning for ways to get out of the predicament she now found herself in. Even though she didn't say anything, didn't deny it, defend it, or fess up to it, this was one of those silent moments where no words were needed. It was a potpourri of truth, clarity, understanding, and compassion. From that day forward, we both could breathe a little easier.

These kinds of moments in my life are exhilarating for me. It's interesting what moves each of us. For some, it's viewing a spectacular landscape, for others, getting a thrill out of adventures like skydiving, and for others still, reading a book they can't put down. For me, it's the insights and epiphanies where everything comes together and makes sense. It's like the proverbial missing piece of the puzzle that tells the complete story. In that moment, all self-doubt is erased, and what I know, I know for sure. Sheer liberation.

I reminded myself of two things as I remembered this breakthrough after moving to be close to my mother. The first was that my burdens became burdens when I assumed responsibility for others. The second was that it never was, never is, and never will be, my responsibility for the choices my mother made in her life that caused her unhappiness.

To support forgiveness for your mother, I encourage you to recognize that while the choices she made negatively affected you, you're not responsible for cleaning up her messes. Yes, you're a part of her journey, but you didn't create those messes; she did. However, if you want to live a happy life, it's imperative you understand that she's reacting to what is, instead of how things should be or could be. Just like you are. Remember, no one is wrong. Everyone sees things from their perspective.

STEP FOUR: ALLOW YOUR MOTHER TO HAVE RESENTMENT TOO.

It's important to understand that your mother is human. She's been impacted by her life circumstances and those have created toxic feelings such as fear, guilt, worry, resentment, and hatred. Anyone who's made to feel bad and wrong about themselves is capable of anything, including the unthinkable. I ask that you imagine life from her point of view. This isn't to make excuses for her, but instead, to gain clarity for you.

It's time to pull out your journal. You're now armed with a new understanding about your mother's past and how it's affected her then and now. Before you write, please summon compassion for where you are emotionally. Validate your feelings. When you feel ready, consider these questions: Based on your newfound knowledge and understanding of your mother, how does it change your thoughts about her now that you know she sees the world from a different perspective than you do? How might this change your relationship dynamic? Gaining clarity around how your perspectives differ may allow your heart to open—even just a little bit. Remember, not accepting your mother means you're not fully accepting yourself. To live a life that you love, you must stop resisting and judging where you came from.

I acknowledge you for your willingness and courage to take on this exploration. It will serve you greatly.

Chapter 5

UNDERSTANDING HER JOURNEY

Your mother is a woman first, a mother second.

Many years ago, I was driving to my uncle's funeral. I was having difficulty finding the burial site despite doing my best to follow the map I'd been given. The cemetery was so large, I was afraid I wouldn't make it in time for the service. Finally, I spotted a procession of cars parking alongside the road and saw my cousins walking on the grass.

I parked my car and hurried along to catch up with my family and friends who were now gathered together at the burial site. In my haste, my heel got stuck in the muddy soil, and I fell to my knees. I was face-to-face with a tombstone. I couldn't help but notice that the woman buried there had been born and had died on the same day of the same month, eighty years apart. I found this fascinating because I believe that the day we're born and the day we die mean something significant. I've looked for this phenomenon since then, but I haven't seen it.

The date of my mother's death, September 7, 2018, wasn't even close to her birth date of February 19, 1928. She wished to be cremated, and her cremains rest in a beautiful urn covered with flowers and butterflies in a special spot in my home.

Even though I'll never forget the day my mother passed, I believe she died many years earlier. I often say that my mother dodged a lot of bullets in her lifetime. I still wonder which one was responsible for killing her spirit. Maybe it was losing her father at the tender age of nine. Her mother was left to financially support the children, both my mother and her older brother, which left her little time for nurturing them.

Just as likely, I predict it was the year 1944, when the Nazis occupied Hungary and my mother became separated from her mother and brother, who chose her safety over theirs. Once the news broke out that the Nazis were invading homes, a loving, Christian friend, who risked her own life to help my mother out, concealed her in a large wheel barrel underneath potatoes and covered it with a heavy burlap tarp. She managed to safely transport my mother to a temple that was partially destroyed by the Nazis the day before. She heard rumors that other Jews were hiding out there. My mother spent the night safely with the others that were concealed there, until they were captured early the next morning and taken off to camps. My mother was transported to a Labor Camp where she remained until the war ended one year and three months later. She had no knowledge of her family's whereabouts or what the future would bring.

As horrific as this story is, I believe there's one other that's a strong contender that's responsible for changing who my mother was at a core level. This one happened during her time at the Labor Camp. She shared the next story with me when I was in my late twenties and told it so nonchalantly and devoid of emotion that she could have been sharing the latest episode of The Oprah Winfrey Show.

"One day," she said, "I was working in a field when three Russian soldiers approached me. I didn't speak Russian and didn't understand what they were saying, but they were laughing and appeared friendly. I was fifteen and a virgin. They took turns raping me." She didn't know why they didn't kill her after they finished. It's unlikely my mother would ever forget this trauma. It's even more unlikely that she'd take the time to make sense of why it happened. Given that Jews were literally being hunted down and transported to the death camps at that time also meant she couldn't even feel secure about the future.

After the war ended, my mother eventually reunited with her mother and brother who were also spared. They spent some time in Austria before emigrating to New York. During this time, my mother met my father in a restaurant. There was a contest where the men were asked to buy a ticket for the *prettiest* woman and my father paid for ten tickets in honor of my mother. They dated briefly before my father left to search for surviving family members. My mother and her family turned their attention to securing the necessary papers for passage to America.

When my mother, her mother, and brother arrived in New York, cousins who'd settled in Far Rockaway, New York in the Queens borough welcomed them. These cousins had made the wise decision to flee Hungary at the first talk of war. My mother's aunt and uncle opened their home to my mother's family, and that's where they remained for a few years.

My mother was fond of my father and hoped they'd reunite someday. And as destiny would have it, a few years after settling in New York, a mutual friend of theirs told my mother's aunt that my father was living close by. My aunt hosted a reunion dinner and persuaded my parents to marry soon after that.

My father, who was Romanian, was also captured during the war. He was sent to a labor camp where his auto mechanic skills meant he spent much of his time in the camp working on Nazi army trucks. His talents made him valuable to the Nazis and were probably why his life was spared.

Though he was valuable to the Nazis, this didn't translate to a less harsh life for my father, and he formulated a plan to escape. His plan was brilliant, and it required a lot of courage. He'd work on a truck he knew would be leaving the camp that day. As it grew dark, he'd lift himself up and hold on to the undercarriage, being careful so he wouldn't be seen. It was a dangerous plan; for if caught, he'd be killed immediately. As he'd hoped, a Nazi soldier climbed into the cab, turned the key, and drove out of the camp unaware that he had "extra" cargo. When the soldier stopped on the side of a deserted road to sleep for the night, my father quietly made his way across the road in the dark to a cornfield where he hid until morning. It was a miracle that he survived the cold night. In the morning, he walked through the cornfields until he came across a small village. He was on the verge of collapsing from hunger and exhaustion. He feared being seen because of the telltale yellow star on his shirt that identified him as a Jew. If the wrong person saw him, it was a certainty that he'd be captured and killed. Instead, he was found by a kind, elderly man who wrapped his coat around my father and took him to his home. He gave my father shelter and food and nursed him until he was strong again. The war ended one month later.

Shortly thereafter, my father learned that his mother and young sister had perished, but he was thrilled to learn that his brother and some friends had survived. He made the trip to New York with them and unknowingly settled near where my mother lived. The rest, as they say, is history. My mother was just shy of twenty years old when they married.

I know my parents loved each other very much. But the trauma they lived through lived on within them. They didn't seek therapy. They handled things on their own as was the way of their generation. Feelings and emotions weren't considered important. Surviving and making a living was what they focused on. Everything else was unimportant.

By the time they celebrated their six-year wedding anniversary, their discordant relationship was showing its effects: they weren't happy. My mother considered leaving my father, but he convinced her to stay, promising that having children was the answer. Three years later, and after a couple of miscarriages, my sister and I were born.

As I grew older, I wished my parents would divorce because they were two good people who deserved to be happy. My father did his best to control everything and didn't consider how unhappy he was. I know in my heart that he was a great man, and I loved him very much.

He worked hard and provided for his family. We never went without food, shelter, or a good education. In his later years, he became financially sound and provided many luxuries for us. Yet, his abusive behavior was a constant in our lives and revealed how he'd turned the trauma he'd lived through into deep and lasting self-hatred. My sister and I couldn't see this link, nor did we have the capacity to understand it. We were emotionally underdeveloped. What we needed was our parents' love.

As I gathered together information about my mother's early life, I was surprised to learn from my grandmother that my mother studied ballet as a young girl and was believed to have a promising future as a ballerina. A puzzle piece clicked into place. I remembered how happy my mother was when she attended the ballets at Lincoln Center. She practically beamed! I remembered, as a young teenager, yelling at my mother to *turn it down!* as she blasted opera music throughout the house. Everyone who knew my mother knew how much she loved culture and the arts. Music was her escape. All her despair would wash away as she listened to a good symphony or watched a Broadway musical, an opera, or a ballet. She was an avid reader and could read an entire book in one or two days. She knew a little bit about everything.

As amazing as it was that my mother survived her circumstances and found some interests in life, she wasn't spared the deep scars. When I think about which experience had the greatest impact—or whether cumulatively all of them were responsible for killing her spirit—I believe there was a moment when she made the decision that she wasn't worth the space she took up in the world. If my mother had a tombstone, I'd imagine three dates engraved below her name. The first would be her date of birth. Next, would be the date her spirit was killed. Finally, the last date would be the day she died.

The trauma my mother lived through and the negative self-image she carried wasn't only a recipe for an unhappy life, it was a predictable disaster for becoming an emotionally unavailable and neglectful mother. I strongly believe that any of us who live through trauma and seek healing can recover and live happy lives. The scars, however, will forever remain. For those who don't address their emotional wellness, an even greater tragedy occurs as those scars remain open wounds. My mother's decision not to seek therapy ensured that she wouldn't be a nurturing caretaker for herself or her future children.

In making peace with my mother during the last few years of her life, I grew to understand why she was incapable of mothering me in the way that I needed her to. Today, I'm angrier still knowing that it wasn't just me who was robbed of my mother. My mother was stripped of a happy life, too. And the world at large missed out on who she was as a talented woman. I often wonder what she would have become had she reached her potential for greatness, if she'd lived under different circumstances. I remain super angry about those of us who dim our light because we've suffered greatly. That's truly tragic and why I believe the world needs all the help it can get.

One regret I do live with is that I didn't tell my mother how proud I was of her while I had the opportunity. But truth be told, I didn't fully connect those dots until I was writing my speech for her memorial service. Recognizing my mother's tremendous value as a survivor will always be a source of comfort for the little girl inside of me who yearned to have *all* of her mother, not just small glimpses of who she could be.

STEP FIVE: FINDING COMPASSION FOR THE LIFE SHE LIVED.

To forgive someone, we must find compassion for what they lived through that made them who they are. Compassion isn't a tool used to rationalize or justify their behavior, but instead to understand that they carry deep wounds that changed their innocence and heart. Seeing your mother as a woman instead of *your mother* will help in this process. As difficult as it may be, it's time to objectively examine your mother's journey with fresh eyes. If your mother hasn't shared her life with you, do some research. If there are relatives or friends you feel comfortable talking to, ask them to share what they know.

Next, instead of putting yourself in *her* shoes, put yourself in *her* life. Often, I believe when we *step into another's shoes,* we're still judging them from where we believe their perspective lies. That viewpoint isn't accurate because we each perceive situations differently. We don't see things in the same way. We don't all come to the same conclusions, see the same options, or make the same choices.

When I imagine myself *living* my mother's life, I'm certain I would have been searching for the tallest bridge to jump off. As I documented some of their memories in this book, I cried knowing that my parents lived through such atrocities. I fully believe I couldn't have handled the trauma she lived through. What interests me immensely though and brings me great pride is recognizing that her trauma is alive in me, too. Even though I didn't live through her experiences, they live through me. This transference of experience explains a lot of my fears that can sometimes seem irrational. But when I think about what my mother lived through my fears make perfect sense. I'm hypersensitive to using security systems at all times in my home, super protective of my belongings, and have a fear of going hungry. If you consider the Holocaust and all that was threatened in my mother's life, and having her experiences live on in my DNA, it makes perfect sense that I'd have these sensitivities. That's why I believe it's so helpful and supportive to reveal as much of your mother's journey as possible so you can see her objectively as a woman. The only way to open up to compassion for someone you resent and feel has wronged you is to remove the *need and the longing*, the expectations you have as her child, and see her as a woman who *isn't* your mother.

Document in your journal the information you find and how you believe you would have felt and reacted to the circumstances she faced. I can say with conviction that as I write this book, I'm blown away with how my mother survived any of it. In the next chapter,

I'll discuss how my view of my mother changed dramatically once I understood the woman she was before becoming a mother.

As you reveal your mother's journey, be kind and compassionate with yourself. The next step will be uncovering your views about your life.

Be proud and acknowledge yourself for everything you're doing to change your relationship with yourself and your mother.

I've included the speech I read at my mother's memorial because it shows the magnitude of the shifts that happen when we forgive. I keep it close, and I read it often.

> **My Dearest Mom,**
>
> **I could not imagine how much I would miss you. I knew that you lived longer than I expected and so I felt with certainty that our time was limited.**
>
> **In the last few years, I have grown to love you and appreciate you in only the ways I prayed to God that a daughter can feel for her Mother.**
>
> **I can say that for way too long, I've misjudged you, minimized your courage, your strength, and your selflessness to navigate life with an acceptance that many strive for and most never reach. I respect your journey, and I honor my own.**
>
> **Thank you for giving me life and for being my greatest teacher.**
>
> **I always believed I needed you to be proud of me. I see now that I needed to be proud of you. I am so proud of you.**
>
> **I will live in honor of you always. Know that the betterment I create in the world is a legacy to you.**

I see you happy and free, blowing me kisses, and me sending them back.

And I trust that the chocolate in heaven is far better than anything here.

I love you so much.

Your loving daughter,
Eve

Chapter 6

REVEALING YOUR STORY

When you're butting heads with your mother, you're trapped in your story. It's time to step out.

"Boy, were you screwed!"

My teacher and mentor, the late Debbie Ford, abruptly interrupted me with a shout. We were on a phone session, and I was recalling a childhood memory.

Initially, I was confused by Debbie's reaction and what it meant about me and my life at the time. I finally made the connection through an epiphany later on. Even though none of my experiences were horrific in and of themselves, I suffered consistent and constant emotional abuse daily. I was traumatized in small doses over prolonged periods of time.

When I recalled childhood memories, there wasn't any specific event that would justify the way I was feeling. Nothing seemed outrageous to me. When I'd hear others describe the horrific transgressions inflicted on them, my life experiences paled in comparison. So, I'd judge myself and minimize my feelings, brushing them off by deciding my sensitivity was the culprit. There was even a time where I wondered whether I had repressed a memory too painful to acknowledge. I didn't fully understand that what I experienced was a slow, continuous emotional and mental destruction of my spirit. It made sense that I was depressed, although I couldn't connect it at the time. Instead,

I decided Debbie was right; I was screwed. Later, I concluded that my parents were screwed, too! Big time!

The abuse that my father inflicted on me and my sister was anything but subtle. He began playing mind games when we were just five years old and didn't ever really stop, even after we were decades away from childhood. He'd say things and then later deny he'd said them, renege on monetary allowances, laugh and exploit things that I'd say or do, and trick me into believing that I was crazy. He impressed on me and my sister that we were spoiled, wrong, overly sensitive crybabies when he didn't get his way, we disagreed with him, or we reacted to his offenses. He was a master at pitting each member of the family against each other by trying to control everyone.

Like my mother, we loved and feared my father. But as I grew older, I came to resent my mother even more than him. I resented her for being such a bad role model, not protecting us, and instilling in us that it's okay to be treated badly by others.

As a child, I became anxious about remembering things I'd learned because at any time, out of nowhere, my father would pose questions that I didn't always know the answers to. He'd shame me when I gave the wrong answer. I couldn't help but notice the pleasure on his face when he got to *be right* about how *wrong* I was. My mother, often present for the mental and emotional abuse, sat quietly by his side or washed dishes in the sink nearby.

I was overly criticized and told directly, "You won't amount to anything successful," and "Thank goodness you're pretty and should find a nice man to take care of you." The constant berating began to wear me down. He'd add more confusion by stressing how important having an education was and insisting that I had to go to college. Surprisingly, he paid for my college tuition. But after I graduated and landed a job in New York, both parents insisted I couldn't take care of myself, and I should marry quickly. By now, I had bought into their view of me as wrong as it was. I lived in constant fear. I developed a strong dependence on others for emotional and financial support.

It's no wonder my relationships became predictably codependent and strained.

During my early impressionable years, my mother was my father's prime target, and I felt sorry for her. But as I grew into a young adult, I lost respect for her. I couldn't understand how she could put up with my father and allow her children to endure abuse. Today, I recognize that she was complicit by not protecting us and putting a stop to it. I also understand now that it's up to me to seek healing and give myself the emotional support I didn't get from them.

My mother always defended my father. In their later years together, he became extra nasty toward her. He even bought a house to live in by himself. My mother wasn't allowed to have a key. Yet, she always took his side by insisting, "Your father may not be a mushy, warm man. He had a terrible childhood, and he doesn't mean any harm. He loves us very much." I don't think she fully understood that even though they didn't divorce, he abandoned her in the end. Despite how he treated her, she still defended him even after his sudden death at age eighty-eight. I believe they stayed way too long in a bad relationship. They both deserved better.

My impression of my mother was that she was a weak, helpless woman, who chose to lay herself out as a doormat and let others walk all over her. *I'll never become like her.* That thought consumed me much of the time. I grew to resent her for being such a bad role model and for not guiding her children toward success.

The more I remembered my childhood and revealed my judgments toward my mother, the more sense Debbie Ford's reaction to the memory I shared with her made. Back then, I believed I'd never reach the happiness I longed for because I was damaged beyond repair. It wasn't until my healing journey began that I could see that I blamed my parents for what was wrong in my life. I finally understood that as long as I continued to hold on to the resentment, I'd never be happy.

I began to gather information about the thoughts, beliefs, and insecurities I'd struggled with throughout my life. Two things struck me:

1) I was preoccupied by constant negative thoughts, and 2) There was a pattern to my experiences. The experiences I was attracting matched my mindset. *What you think about, you bring about.*

Soon, I identified a list of negative beliefs that remained constant throughout my life. This supported me to expose the *story* I carried around with me wherever I went. The early decisions I made about my parents, the poor self-image I created about myself, and the deep emotions I felt about the neglect in my life were all bringing forth experiences to confirm that I wasn't good enough, I didn't matter, I wasn't lovable, and I would never be happy. The list was long and grim.

When we're young children, we're innocent, full of wonder, impressionable, and curious. We do what we can to make sense of everyone and everything around us. Through our relationships and experiences, we make conclusions about things that then support us in making decisions about how to think, feel, and behave. Because our goal is to survive, avoid punishment, and attain love and approval, we'll do whatever we believe will bring us what we need.

When our beliefs about ourselves and others are negative, we then fall into the victim role believing that life is unfair, we don't matter, and we won't prosper. Because we're thinking it, we begin attracting it. For many, the next step is resigning to life just not being fair or good to them. Before long, we master strategies and coping skills to keep us safe. And too often, we sabotage our circumstances because we hate who we are. Predictably, our experiences match our impression, and we continue to suffer and struggle.

Despite what was happening around me, I was able to create a picture in my mind of a loving family as a young child. I needed to believe that my parents loved and cared about me even when all evidence contradicted my fantasy.

I developed great, albeit unhealthy coping skills in my twenties. Various substances helped me dull my feelings. But in my thirties, when I cleaned up my act and chose to live a healthier life, my denial about my life broke down. I knew I needed support and went into therapy.

My therapist helped me to expose and face the darker truths about my life that I'd worked so hard to suppress. My deeper beliefs were reaching the surface, and they were painful. It became clear that my then marriage was built on those suppressed beliefs. I made the decision to leave my marriage. After my divorce, when I summoned up the courage to get back out in the dating field, I was stumped when asked the question, "What's your story?"

I laugh about this question now, because back then my story had to do with the details in my life. I would run off a dossier in my mind about the details of my childhood: where I grew up, where I went to camp, where I attended school. I'd mention that I was a twin, and that my parents had emigrated from Eastern Europe. These details weren't wrong, but unaware of it back then, they didn't explain who I was, which was further evidence that *I had no idea who I was*.

In therapy, I was encouraged to blame my parents. It felt good for a while to do that. But over time, the negative victim story I revealed remained very much alive. I had no proactive measures to move me forward. My sessions were forty-five minutes of an angry rant about what he or she did. And often, I'd leave more depressed at the end of the session.

I wanted to feel better and investigated alternate ways to learn and heal. I purchased many books from the self-improvement section of bookstores and became an avid reader. I felt comforted by what I read and felt hopeful that there was a light at the end of the dark tunnel. But still, I was living deeply within my own perspective of things.

Any time I got together with my parents, even after I was well into my fifties, I'd step into *my story* firmly with both feet. In their presence, all my limiting beliefs were triggered. I felt the *trapped* feelings of my childhood when there was no escaping the experience. These feelings made it impossible for me to see my parents in any other way than who I believed them to be. I was living the belief that they didn't support or care about me. A simple stare or snide comment from my father or an unprovoked thought in my head would send me thinking, judging, and spiraling down into my *they don't love me* story. And, because they weren't warm and loving, I was convinced (again!) that I was cheated out of the loving parents every child deserves.

It was during my first predictable, emotionally abusive marriage in my late twenties that I understood that my parents were clueless as to how their poor parenting and bad relationship had affected me. When I tried talking to them about my strained marriage, they couldn't or wouldn't see the abuse I was suffering. Instead, they encouraged me to stay. Feelings and emotions weren't important in my parents' marriage, so why should it be any different for their children? What I found most interesting was that even though I was miserable in my relationship with my husband, a short visit with them had me believe that my relationship wasn't so bad. *At least I'm not them living in their lives!* This thought helped me to rationalize and justify my circumstances while keeping me firmly in *my story* and in the dysfunction of my relationship. I was sabotaging my opportunities for happiness.

On my journey toward forgiveness, it was important for me to understand that my parents did what they knew. They couldn't be the parents I needed because they lacked the self-love necessary to nurture another. They didn't have their own backs, and they hardly supported each other in a loving way. They were only capable of being caretakers, nothing more. I was so firmly planted in my story that I was unable to see their reality objectively.

By the time I reached high school, I was rather good at wearing the *I've got it all together* mask that hid my insecurities well, especially from myself. This attitude had an interesting result that helped me get noticed by my classmates. My popularity was my saving grace, but it also helped me hide. I became so good at hiding that I fooled even myself. But deep down, my beliefs kept playing the same records: *I'm unlovable, I'm a loser, I don't belong anywhere, no one supports me, I can't take care of myself.* These themes were in the driver's seat of my life. They impacted my choices and attracted negative experiences that left me feeling hopeless, angry, and frustrated.

In my mid-forties, I hit rock bottom after my second divorce. My insecurities and fear got the best of me, and I developed panic attacks. I thought something was wrong with everyone around me, and I became scared of everyone and everything. I was seriously concerned that if I didn't get the proper help soon, I'd become too afraid to go outside. I had to stop working and relied on savings to live. I blamed my parents for my harsh reality and felt completely abandoned. They didn't know what panic attacks were, and they didn't want to learn. They didn't try to understand or offer any compassion or support when I talked to them about my struggle. It was during this time that I began referring to my parents when I spoke of them to others, as *Spirit Crushers*.

My parents never struck me, but my spirit took a heavy blow, regardless. I suffered significantly both emotionally and mentally. I developed a very negative self-image. And yet, even though I had enough evidence to prove that I'd never receive the love I so yearned for from them, I didn't stop trying. Time after time, I'd be let down. But the next time I was feeling low, I'd reach out to my mother, in hopes of catching a glimpse of compassion, some motherly love, or a helpful word of advice. I usually left our conversations feeling worse.

In the last years of my mother's life, I discovered that my need for the mother I longed for conflicted with the mother I had. I could see that we both lived in our stories, which were littered with shattered hopes and dreams. Neither of us was making any effort to improve our relationship. When we point our fingers at another person as being the reason we're suffering, the last thing we do is take responsibility for our own behavior. We wait, instead, for them to change. I don't think I have to spell out the chances of that happening in our favor.

One day, a friend visiting from New York joined my mother and me for lunch. As we chatted, my mother brought up my birth story, one I'd heard many times. For some reason, on this particular day, I felt myself growing angry as I listened. When I could listen no longer,

I excused myself and headed for the ladies' room where, through focused breathing, I was able to calm myself down. Aside from the fact that my mother was repeating herself more these days as her dementia worsened, something else was at play that I couldn't quite put my finger on. So, I did what I do when I feel clueless; I prayed to God to show me what I wasn't seeing.

Ask and ye shall receive! Later that day as I sat in my office, I was blindsided by an epiphany. It came after asking, "Why am I so upset every time my mother tells the story about my birth? And why today, am I triggered more than ever?" I asked these questions out loud a few times. I then thought angrily, *If I hear that story one more time, I'm going to puke!* Still, I was committed to getting answers.

My mind drifted to the details of the story, as I remember my mother telling it, about the day she delivered her children. "It was the greatest joy of my life," my mother would say, beaming like a Cheshire cat. "My two beautiful twin girls! Me and my husband were hoping for a boy, and we had no idea we were having twins. I was put on bedrest for seven months due to the miscarriages I had with other pregnancies. My delivery was particularly painful, and there were no epidurals or pain relief like they have today. Judy was breach born. A beautiful healthy girl. The doctor left the room while the nurses attended to me and my daughter. I was still in a lot of pain, and that's when the nurse realized there was another baby coming. That's when Eve was born, feet first too! My two beautiful girls! I was the proudest mother ever!" As I sat in my office contemplating the mystery of the angry reaction I had had earlier, and asking God for guidance, I was ready to reveal my truth.

Because my mother wasn't demonstratively warm and affectionate, I didn't feel her love. When she'd tell our birth story, exuding joy with every word, I couldn't relate to it. She sounded inauthentic and phony to me. So, when I was subjected to hearing it, I wanted to scream, "It's a lie!" I was embarrassed that my mother would deceive everyone with her tale. People would "Ooh" and "Aah" as they listened while I was preoccupied with my experience of her as a mother. Here she was, disguised as the proud mother of the century while I knew the real mother; detached, unaffectionate, and unwilling to take any responsibility.

Even giving a hug was impossible for her. Her cold demeanor meant my hugs weren't returned. Her arms would remain firmly at her sides. Sometimes, I'd pick up her arms as if to mold them around my waist. She'd quickly disengage and pull them back. When I try to remember any attempts on her part to bond with me, only two scenarios come to mind. One was pushing food on me, which I resented, because she would insist I was too thin. She was quite overweight at times, even obese. As much as she beamed when people complimented her children, deep down I believe she was more jealous than proud. The second way she reached out was suggesting I join her to watch TV. When I agreed, we'd watch together in silence. It was hardly a bonding experience.

Having this clarity about my reaction, I wondered what her personal need was to keep retelling this story. *What kind of person tells a story over and over again? Even before she was showing signs of dementia, she told the story hundreds of times! Why?* Then, bam! Another epiphany! The answer was obvious: A person who needs to convince themselves that what they're saying is true! This answer made perfect sense. She was trying to convince herself that her children were worth all the agony she suffered in her marriage and made up for all her bad choices.

Even though I can't speak for my mother's feelings and intentions, this revelation became a truth that brought me comfort. My newfound understanding of her motivations supported my compassion for her. It couldn't have been easy raising children when you're trapped in a bad marriage. Becoming a mother isn't a job you can decide you don't like and then give two weeks' notice to your boss.

Perhaps my mother's need to tell our birth story was her way of claiming her life had value and that she was happy. It was a way for her to make sense of her life, the choices she made, and the decisions she had to live with. It was how she accepted the life she'd resigned herself to and lessen the pain of the loss of her hopes and dreams for a better life. She rationalized her way to feeling better despite her unhappiness. My mother created a *story* about her life. And, like many of us do to avoid the pain, she glossed over things so she could feel safe.

It was so liberating to have this newfound wisdom to support me in my relationship with myself and my mother. I made a note in my journal, and I chanted a new mantra in service of ending our dysfunction, "Every time my mother steps into her story, I step into mine. It's time to stop!"

In every relationship we attract and engage in, particularly with our most intimate connections such as our family of origin, we'll be provoked from time to time by how we experience their behavior. This happens because we judge these people the most. We have the most personal investments with them, and we have expectations that aren't always rational. We'll always have more reactivity in relationships where we depend on others for love, approval, and financial and emotional support because we depend on these people to give us something we need or desire.

When we butt heads or feel uncomfortable, our thoughts and emotions spiral and we question what it all means. Often, we're left with resentment for them and ourselves. These thoughts, beliefs, and emotions are *our story*. Pay attention next time you get into an argument or disagreement with someone. You can be sure that as the tensions escalate, that you'll both step into a familiar personal story. Each reaction will be indicative of this. It's like traveling back in time to incidents that liken what you're feeling in the present moment. We unconsciously recall and remember the times that were hurtful and carry them into the moment. This would explain why we "overreact" to things. It's not that our response doesn't fit what's happening at the time, it's that our reaction is triggered by the story we live in and carry with us wherever we go.

Since our personalities are formed by the impressions we take in when we're young, we attempt to make sense of everything we experience. We're constantly searching for meaning and to explain why we're here. We have an innate desire to matter and impact others. Our choices and actions are driven by this need. We don't always act in our best interest and, instead, react with old, outdated beliefs, and strategies. As Albert Einstein once said, "The definition of insanity is doing the same thing over and over again and expecting different results."

When we revisit our stories, it's like becoming insane in that moment. We react to our present circumstances based on past conditioning. We then allow fear to run the show and behave as if we're trapped in an original version of the victim story we created. The feelings are real. This behavior happens when someone pushes your buttons, and you react in a predictable way, even if it's only in your mind. This *story* is our truth, created by the way we saw things early on in life. Much like a vow, our story is sacred. But, because our story is old, outdated, and limiting, not to mention written by an emotionally underdeveloped child, it no longer serves the adult. In fact, clinging to an old story will have disastrous results. Case in point: It took three divorces before I understood this fact.

When my mother and I butted heads, we were immersed in our own stories, which didn't mesh. She had her version of life, and I had mine. Both of us were living in our own stories, which made it unlikely our expectations of each other would ever be met.

A few months after my mother passed away, I contacted Hollister Rand, a well-known Los Angeles-based medium and author. I've believed in the spirit world for many years and feel comforted that professionals who are able to transmit information from deceased loved ones exist. When Hollister delivered a communication from my mother, I almost fell out of my chair.

"Your mother wants you to know that she was profoundly unhappy and never wanted to be a mother. But she needs you to know that she has always loved you and your sister. She is also urging me to tell you that she never healed from her trauma during the war and is at peace now. She is willing to be the mother you didn't have back then, now." I felt the tears streaming down my face as Hollister shared my mother's message. I also felt validated and comforted in a way I can't fully put into words.

"Are you willing to let your mother be a mother to you now?" Hollister asked me.

"Gosh," I said. "I feel my mother's presence a lot, but never once did I consider that she can be the mother I always needed."

"If you invite her to, she will." Hollister assured me.

In a later chapter, I'll share more about my relationship with my mother today, with me residing here on this planet and her in the spirit world. It's truly remarkable.

STEP SIX: DISCOVER YOUR STORY AND TAKE A STEP OUT.

This is a good time to make a list of the thoughts and beliefs that feel familiar to you in your journal. I'm specifically referring to negative, limiting thoughts that feel hurtful, uncomfortable, and dark. Examples of these are: "I'm not good enough." "The world isn't safe." "I don't fit in." "I'm a loser." "No one supports me." "The world isn't safe." "I'll end up alone."

The thoughts we carry that were developed early in our lives have become part of our conditioning and the way we see ourselves, others, and the world. It may feel uncomfortable or scary to bring these to the surface, so I encourage you to be kind and compassionate toward yourself as you do this exercise. We can't change anything we aren't aware of and that we don't acknowledge. Exposing some of your negative beliefs will give you a glimpse into your *story,* so it's worth summoning up your willingness and courage to spend some time exploring.

Negative thinking is more powerful than positive thinking when it comes to making our choices in life. Fear can easily run the show and keep us paralyzed and unable to go after what we want. Discovering the thoughts and beliefs you carry will support you in the forgiveness process, too, because you need to find love and compassion for yourself. Self-forgiveness is the bigger goal here.

Make two columns in your journal. In one column, make a list of at least twenty beliefs you have. Remember to not judge yourself or beat yourself up. We're aiming for compassion and love here, not animosity and resentment. In the next column, write down the decisions you made as a result of each belief. See the following example.

Example:

BELIEFS	DECISION
I'm not good enough.	I must make everyone happy so that they'll like me.
Life isn't fair.	I won't have any expectations.
No one supports me.	I must do everything myself.

Keep in mind that your beliefs arose over time. First, they were mere thoughts that came from experiences you had. Next, you began thinking them incessantly, turning them into conditioned beliefs. The decisions you've made because of these beliefs help to carve the *themes* that run through your story. Our themes guide our behavior and responses to our experiences to compensate for the negative way we feel.

Once you've uncovered your *story*, understand that your mother has her story, too. Know that when you're with your mother, or think about your mother, you probably dip into your story to make your present experiences familiar and predictable.

Changing your behavior to stop running your story with your mother requires a commitment and willingness to embark on this step. As you step outside of your story, be kind and supportive of yourself. What you're doing isn't easy. Know that to *step out* you must first acknowledge that you've fully stepped into the past and the old conditioning. When you become aware of this old pattern, you can simply tell yourself, "I'm in my old story, and it's safe to step out." All that's required is a shift in perception. You're also in a better position to ask yourself, "What just happened that took me back into the past?" What behavior from the other person triggered your initial response?

Being objective in the present moment also offers you the ability to tell someone that their behavior is no longer acceptable to you. Instead of becoming emotionally upset and attacking them (which won't serve you), you can say, "Hey, it's not okay to say that to me." Once you connect with why something triggered you, you can take a deep breath and choose to react to what's happening from an objective point of view instead of reverting to the past. Learning to do this will take time and practice.

The purpose of revealing your *story* and understanding that your mother holds her own *story* is to reveal the dynamic that governs your relationship with her. When you consciously choose to *step out* of your story, you can objectively see things differently. If you want to live a happy life and get along with people, this exercise will support you to live in peace instead of projection. Always remember that the qualities we don't like about ourselves are those we won't tolerate with others. And very often, we'll butt heads with the people whose beliefs mirror ours. It's our different expressions that have us believe no one hears or understands us.

Again, be kind and compassionate with yourself as you expose your *story*. The next time you think about your mother, and you have a negative thought or feeling, practice *stepping out*.

Chapter 7

THE PURPOSE OF FORGIVENESS

To forgive isn't for them, it's your right to a happy life despite them.

"I'm so sorry. Can you forgive me?"
"You forgive me, right? I mean, we're good. Right?"
Many powerful words in our vocabulary carry great meaning, both negative and positive: fear, hate, love, peace. You could add forgiveness to that list, too. "I forgive you," is a loaded concept that's thrown around these days as readily as the phrase, *I love you.* We're more casual than ever with our communications, the messages we send, the offense we enable, and the bad behavior we reward. It's evident in the way we treat each other. There's a lack of boundary-setting and the absence of consequences. We talk a lot, send mixed messages, and contradict what we say by what we do or don't do. Have we forgotten we all deserve respect?

We say we want more connected, meaningful relationships, but our actions indicate that we'd much rather avoid confrontations and pain at all costs and get back to *feeling good.* The problem, I believe, is that in our quest for happiness, we're stepping over important indicators that we're on a futile path, blame everyone around us for the discomfort we feel, and justify and rationalize to manipulate the circumstances for the outcome we want. Are we sweeping transgressions under the rug too quickly without considering the offense? If so, then why are we so bewildered when things don't work out? *How did I end up here again?* has become a common question for many. Do we not see there's a pattern here? Everyone talks about addressing the common denominator in all our experiences. Well, that's just part of the solution. We must see the common behavior too. We are part of the equation that creates the circumstances we attract.

I believe that forgiveness plays a huge role in our ability to attract healthy relationships and, even more so, our perception of what forgiveness is and how it will benefit our lives, is key if we want to live a happy life. And, it particularly affects the relationship we have with ourselves. As *A Course in Miracles* states, "Forgiveness is the key to happiness." I love the quote so much I had it painted on the wall in my home. But even after doing that, I didn't fully understand how powerful a part forgiveness plays in our lives and why it wasn't working quite so well for me.

The conversation surrounding forgiveness is amplified in religion, relationships, politics, and the quest for world peace. *We all deserve forgiveness. To be happy, we must forgive.* And then there are those who adamantly stand their ground, "I'll never forgive them for what they've done! No way!" I fell into a *middle ground* but not without stumbling much of the time.

Personally, I've struggled with forgiveness most of my life. As a People Pleaser, I forgave too easily, too readily, and too much. I gave everyone the benefit of the doubt and more than just one "second chance." Early in my life, the concept of forgiveness meant forgetting the transgression and *starting over.* I imagined erasing my feelings much like Mrs. Cankro, my elementary school teacher, who, at the conclusion of class, erased the blackboard with long strokes back and forth, making the lessons of the day transform into a chalky haze on the blackboard. You couldn't read what was once there nor could you retrieve it in its original form. To forget my feelings created a cloud of confusion.

Forgiving others meant I stayed in situations that didn't feel good for way too long. I lacked the ability to set boundaries or implement consequences. Unconsciously, I didn't believe I had choices, options, or any power to do anything about it. One thing I could count on was that I was a *nice* person. I believed that kindness would always prevail. But what lurked deep within my psyche was what I truly thought and felt about people and their behavior. My emotions were boiling over into rage. I may have believed I was forgiving my offenders, but I was really growing angrier by the minute. I was building a long resentment list, and I was at the top of it. *How could I be so stupid! What kind of person forgives that?*

"No one's perfect." "Stand by your man." "Everyone deserves a second chance." "Their intention was good." "We all make mistakes." "Be the better person." These are phrases we say to justify and rationalize the circumstances we attract and cocreate that leave us feeling sad, angry, frustrated, rejected, defeated, and alone. Why do we do this? Because we're taught that everyone deserves to be forgiven no matter what. And, good people forgive.

For now, I'm going to leave God out of this conversation. I'm going to stay firmly planted in my ego mind, on this physical planet, and in my human experience, because it's important to understand forgiveness from this perspective, too. It's important to note why it doesn't work in the way we're conditioned to believe it *should*.

In the past, I believed forgiveness meant a free pass to my offenders, like the "Get out of jail free" card in the game, Monopoly. No matter what someone did or for how long it went on, they deserved to be forgiven, *especially* if they apologized. I, as a kind and generous young woman with a big heart, owed it to them to forgive and forget, despite their betrayal. But deep in my gut, it felt bad, and it felt wrong.

"I forgive you," I'd say. But I didn't. Instead, I pushed down my anger, forced a smile, and built an internal resentment list that would eventually create an outer armor that made me unapproachable. I did this while believing I was nicer than most.

After decades of People Pleasing, I lost my faith in people. I came to fear that others had rights I didn't and that I was unimportant, uninteresting, and unlovable. Before long, despite my ability to see it, I became unloving. I lost faith that *there's good in all of us* and began living a life full of resignation and distrust.

The more I *forgave* others, the more I hated myself, and the more I blamed them. What I didn't realize until much later was that it was me I believed was bad and wrong for feeling the way I did and that, despite my efforts to make everyone happy, I wouldn't find love because I was way too angry and hateful. I also learned that I didn't understand forgiveness back then, although I'm certain I was spot on in receiving the guidance as it had been presented to me. It wasn't that I was crazy, but instead a good student following the directions I was given. These directions required that I disregard my feelings and expression to be a better person for others.

As time went on, I discovered different perspectives on forgiveness and eventually created my personal rules for forgiveness. For me, and many of my clients and friends who were willing to try this new perspective, it works like a charm. Stayed tuned. I'll share it with you too. It changed the way I see myself, others, and the world. It empowers me, excites me, restores hope within me, and helps me to love and protect myself. I have faith in people again but in a different, more sound way. I've become kinder and more generous than I ever could have imagined. Most of all, I've accepted that however I choose to forgive, I matter most in the equation. I'm my primary love interest now and forever.

I could share my forgiveness rules with you here, but I believe a good back story will help to make sense of the nonsense we struggle to make sense of. It's important for you to understand how I reached my conclusions. I won't try to convince you to take on my perspective, but instead hope that you resonate with some aspect of my story. That way, we can crack a window and let in some air. As you feel the breeze caress your face, consider that all you feel is right, even your darkest thoughts, and that you're entitled to all your feelings. It's time to feel them all. And most importantly, you don't have to conform to any majority way of thinking to attain deep meaning for your life; in fact, doing so is more than not, the cause of your struggle. I will say that forgiveness not only works, it heals. And because I've never believed in *one size fits all,* I don't suggest my rules will work for everyone. We're alike but we're also unique. Take what works for you and put the rest aside. If we were to follow our gut as children, kept what worked and threw away what didn't, we wouldn't be pondering the question, "Who am I?" today. We'd feel free to fully express ourselves. As children, though, we're not emotionally developed enough to follow our intuition, and we're at the mercy of others who thrust their misguided conditioning onto us.

I encourage you to make yourself the greatest love interest for the rest of your life. Doing so will bring you joy and help you grow to love others in ways you can't imagine now. Self-love requires you to let go of what ails you in a way that feels right to you and for you. Allow forgiveness into your life and tailor it to suit you. Self-love is the antidote to anything that ails us, and it gives us the ability to protect ourselves against the offenses in the world.

On September 10, 2001, my husband, Brad, and I concluded a fourteen-day trip to Eastern Europe. We landed at New York's Kennedy Airport just after six o'clock in the evening. We finally reached our Upper Eastside apartment around 8:00 p.m.

This trip abroad had been a last-ditch effort to improve my strained marriage, but deep in my heart, I knew it was over. I was sad. I was angry. I was scared.

As I unpacked from our trip, my mind shifted to the new job I'd be starting on the seventeenth. I felt overwhelmed with so many changes happening in my life. I had no idea what the next morning would bring and how my present anxiety was about to reach an all-time high. In just hours, I'd become a woman who no longer felt safe in her life and in the city she once loved. On September 11, 2001, the World Trade Center terrorist attacks changed the world forever, and my life would be rocked to the core.

I knew I was awake, but my eyes resisted opening. I finally glanced at the clock on my night table and was surprised I'd slept so long. I was jet lagged and fell asleep earlier than my usual bedtime. I'd rested undisturbed throughout the night, except for a strange dream about a plane crashing into my high-rise apartment window. I awoke from that dream with a start and found that I was sweating profusely. I spent the next few moments deep breathing and reassuring myself it had been a nightmare. I laid my head back down on my pillow and dozed off. I thought I was dreaming when I heard the phone. I picked it up on the third ring.

"Turn on the news!" my mother demanded. "Now!"

I was annoyed she woke me up from a deep sleep. I was tired and had a few days off before starting my new job. *This better be good,* I remember thinking.

As she waited impatiently on the line, I turned on the television. I couldn't believe what I was seeing and hearing. I sat shocked and horrified as I stared at the television, hoping I was stuck in another nightmare. The World Trade Center was on fire after both towers had been hit by two 767 Boeing aircraft. I recalled my dream the night before and felt terrified. I knew I was wide awake. What I was watching was really happening. I said my goodbyes to my mother and hung up. I then placed a call to Brad, who was already at his job on Long Island. He was watching, too. The world was watching. It was surreal.

As the hours passed, we learned more about the terrorists who had planned the various attacks. Security measures were taken all over the country, including New York. The bridges were closed, and Brad couldn't make it home. I was alone trying to make sense of such an enormous and cruel terrorist attack. I held my dog close and obsessively stayed glued to the television. Today, it seems ludicrous I was preoccupied with the demise of my marriage. But then, in a world that was spiraling out of control, I couldn't imagine myself alone and single again. I was so afraid and felt everything that was happening to me and around me was more than I could bear.

Two weeks later, I started my new job as a leasing agent in a luxury high-rise building downtown in Union Square. It was then that I experienced my first panic attack. I spent many of my first days showing apartments to prospective tenants forced out of their Battery Park homes because of the World Trade Center attacks. Many of the buildings in that area had been deemed unsafe and no one was allowed in. Many people were looking for shelter. There was the undisputable taste of fear in the air.

Frank lived on the top floor of the building. He worked for the firm, Cantor Fitzgerald. He was out of town when the attacks happened. All the people he worked with at his firm who'd showed up for work at the World Trade Center on September 11 had perished. Since all air travel had been grounded on 9/11, Frank wasn't able to return immediately. But, once he received clearance to return home, he spent only a couple of days in his apartment. During a welfare check by the office, it was discovered he'd left for California without breaking his lease. I was told to assess his apartment for any damage and get it cleaned up to get it ready for immediate occupancy.

As I entered the two-bedroom apartment in midafternoon, the sun was streaming in from the west. The views to the south that were once breathtaking were now a reminder of the tragedy downtown. I was stunned at the condition of the apartment. I felt both fear and compassion for the young tenant who'd survived an unthinkable tragedy and returned to face that southern view.

Discarded pizza boxes with old food inside and empty vodka bottles were strewn about. The plastic cups that lined the windowsills were filled with water and cigarette butts. The sludge was now a thick, brown, smelly mess. The carpet in a corner of the living room was partially removed and there were stains everywhere. I wondered what plagued him as he spent his final days in his New York City apartment before abruptly leaving for California. I also wondered how he moved his furniture out of the building without the office knowing. Later, I found out that he'd tipped the doorman five hundred dollars on a Sunday after the leasing office had closed. It took only a couple of hours and three moving trucks to complete the job.

No one could imagine the grief Frank was feeling. His life was spared due to a fluke: a last-minute, out-of-town meeting. I wondered whether his life being spared brought relief or guilt. As I stood in the abandoned apartment, I was consumed with sadness and my eyes welled up with tears. I was comforted by the fact that he wouldn't be financially penalized for leaving. The management granted an exception and released Frank from the obligations of his lease.

I took some notes for the cleaning crew and headed back to my office. While waiting for the elevator, I glanced down at the burgundy carpet with gold diamond shapes. Oddly, the floor seemed to be moving. Simultaneously, I had a sharp pain shoot down both of my arms from my shoulders to my fingertips. I thought I was going to die.

It seemed like an eternity waiting for the elevator to arrive. When the doors finally opened, I stepped inside and leaned against the wall. The heart attack I thought I was having had subsided. I stood there massaging my arms, still in shock. I was grateful there were no other floor stops or passengers. When I reached my office, I made a beeline to the ladies' room and doused my face with cold water. I briefly shared the news with my manager, who insisted I go to the emergency room at the nearest hospital. I chose to go uptown where my doctor was affiliated. I headed out after placing a call to his office.

The emergency room examination didn't reveal anything abnormal, and I was sent home with medication. I booked a follow-up appointment with my doctor for the next day. Before long, I became a regular visitor to his office because my symptoms were getting worse. On most days, I had chest pains, strange head sensations, and dizziness. I thought I was dying all the time. I insisted I be put through all kinds of medical tests. I refused to believe that stress could cause the symptoms I was experiencing. Test after test didn't explain the frightening symptoms I was having. Each time nothing showed up as the culprit, I'd be reduced to tears. I was desperate for answers and couldn't bear going through another day struggling to feel normal. A few months later, my doctor sat me down and explained what was going on.

"Good news. You are healthy and hopefully will live a long life. You're underweight and you're going through life's major stressors. Your marriage is ending, and there was a major terrorist attack in the city where you live and work. I believe once you end your marriage and find a good therapist, you will get better." His words hit home. And, I suppose I was relieved that there wasn't something major wrong with me. It was clear that I had some things I needed to deal with.

By now, Brad had moved out at my insistence and rented an apartment not far away. But I was stalling the divorce. I didn't want to accept that another marriage was over. I was terrified of being a failure and ending up alone forever. But as scared as I was of leaving, I was more afraid of staying in a marriage full of lies and deceit. Fear can be a good motivator sometimes, but in this case, it was keeping me stuck. I mustered up the courage to put the divorce in motion. Brad didn't contest my wishes, and our divorce became final within six months. My doctor was right. I began to feel better and soon weaned myself off my medication. But there was lots more healing to be done.

Today, I equate my struggle and scary physical symptoms to an overwhelming amount of fear and distress. I also determined that I was a sensitive person emotionally and an empath, too. Empaths often experience physical and emotional symptoms by internalizing the experiences of others as if they're going through the experience themselves. So, when New York City was attacked, I was absorbing all sorts of emotions and imagining worst-case scenarios, creating an overload of stimuli. This overload required me to use extra efforts and energies to get through my days and nights. This brought on my panic attacks along with the diagnosis of general anxiety disorder.

Post 9/11, I'd ride the subway believing there was a bomb hidden in someone's knapsack. Each day, I wondered if I'd make it home. I also had a small dog to worry about if I didn't. My mind was filled with horrific scenarios, and I never felt safe. Along with being scared, I had a lot of personal unfinished business in my life and relationships. Things seemed incomplete and unresolved. Even my new job was proving to be disappointing and stressful.

I felt angry at the world, at the terrorists, at my parents, and at Brad. I was disappointed with my friends, my coworkers, and myself. Before long, my mind was preoccupied with who wronged me, how and why it happened, and how naïve and stupid I was to trust people. Life seemed unfair, and my future looked bleak.

Forgiveness was not a concept or a consideration in my life then. In fact, I believed I trusted too easily and forgave people too readily, so I focused on why others were treating me so badly. My anger was gaining momentum, and I wasn't even aware of it. I only knew that I blamed everyone around me for the condition of my life. Soon, I was consumed with hatred. Even under the care of a good therapist, I struggled because our talk sessions didn't provide me any proactive way to channel my anger. In fact, my therapist first encouraged my anger and then made me feel wrong and judged for having the emotion. The agenda was always to get rid of my anger instead of feeling it. So, I continued to stuff down my expression and grew to dislike myself more as a result. I was beating myself up even more. And I always had someone to blame for it. *Thanks, Mom and Dad.*

Because each of us sees the world in our unique way, our perspectives become our reality. It makes sense that we become angry and reactive if fear is running the show, which definitely doesn't make for a happy life. Even so, there was no way I was forgiving the terrorists, my ex-husband who lied and deceived me, my parents who were unsupportive, my coworkers for not wanting to work together as a team, and whoever and whatever else I could find to account for the circumstances in my life that felt like crap. During this time, I watched the news, drank a lot of alcohol, and ate a lot of takeout food. I was finding ways to cope and tune out. And for a time, it seemed as if these things helped me get through the days. At the very least, I was expressing myself. It wasn't gracious, but I felt I was doing what I needed to do at the time.

Eventually, I knew I had to do something differently and was committed to searching for healthier options. As soon as I validated myself and stopped judging myself for making predictable bad choices, I could see other ways of living. Awareness that we're in trouble and acknowledging we need help is essential to produce positive change. I decided my therapist was making things worse, so I began weaning myself by seeing her less. I finally stopped altogether and found needed support and knowledge by skimming books in the self-improvement section of bookstores. I was on a search to find happiness, and I was determined to feel better.

It was time to remove things in my life that weren't bringing me joy. I stopped dating, reduced my alcohol intake, and focused on getting better. I learned about self-love and spiritual teachings, finding them compelling and comforting. They were basic ideals that didn't steer me toward any espoused religion or belief system. Believing in God wasn't mandatory either, which I welcomed since I was angry at him too.

Once I was open to considering there is an unseen force—a higher power—that guides and supports me in every facet of my life, my perspective of things began to shift. These teachings encouraged me to embrace my challenges for the lessons and growth they provided. I was willing to welcome in new and different opportunities and put down my know-it-all hat to heed what I might learn from various teachers. I felt comforted and supported each time I immersed myself in the mindset that *everything happens for a reason* and that even the worst tragedies bring some good. I realized that as long as I was willing to open my eyes and see life differently, I would discover joy.

When I thought about the World Trade Center attacks, I struggled to find any good. In time, I was able to see that some light peeked through the darkness. New Yorkers were bonding in ways they hadn't in the past. Stronger measures for security were being put into place. People were no longer tolerating bad behavior. Even though this didn't make the attacks acceptable, I could understand what these spiritual leaders were suggesting.

When I thought about my latest divorce, I became grateful that I saw things early on instead of investing a lot of time, money, and heart with Brad. My ex-husband taught me important lessons, one in particular, that it's better to leave a bad relationship than to stay a prisoner in one. Of course, this *is the choice my mother made and modeled for me.* It was more loving for both of us to split, despite what happened. We both deserved to be happy.

Several years after embracing my spiritual side, I trained to become an Integrative Life Coach and fell into a *happy trance* as I accepted forgiveness into my life. It was *my way out of hell,* as I called it. I had a yummy feeling inside for people again. My faith was renewed, at least for a while.

During this time, I met and married my third husband, Matt. By now, I was fifty years old. I felt blessed that I had another opportunity to experience a relationship that would bring me connection and joy. Even though Matt wasn't someone I'd consider dating in the past, I felt myself changing, becoming more flexible, and opening to new ways of being. Also, Matt and I had something in common. We were both in the emotional health and wellness field. On a deeper level, though, I felt as if I was pretending much of the time. I couldn't figure out why, but I didn't feel like myself. I felt more distant and detached than ever before. I chalked these feelings up to the newness and unfamiliar practices I was learning. I believed that in time things would fit like a glove.

What I was hiding from myself and others during this time was that I'd discovered a new way to cover up my true feelings and expression. I was living a different version of the same story where others were more important than me, and I had to do whatever I could to make them happy. As before, I believed that love would prevail. Forgiveness felt great, but there was a residual feeling that kept coming up for me whenever I forgave. *I felt like the fool.*

Matt was the perfect teacher for me because he was pushing my buttons all the time. He was also accusing me of seeing circumstances inaccurately and being angry, even when I wasn't being or feeling angry in his presence. I didn't understand how he would get that impression. In my relationship with Matt, I had to gloss over everything. He liked to talk the death out of details while remaining even keeled and calm. He couldn't see how frustrating and provocative he was being. As our discussion would continue, I'd eventually sound frustrated. This triggered him, and he'd get all hot and bothered, wagging a finger at me while saying, "You're so angry!" It drove me crazy! But it also woke me up. The more humiliated and wrong I felt, the more the fight within me stirred.

We made plans to divorce just one month shy of our second anniversary. Matt decided he didn't want to be married anymore and didn't care to work things out. We agreed not to file for divorce for the next six months so that I could benefit from his health insurance. But we didn't wait to separate. We broke our lease and moved to our respective apartments in the same town. I was beginning to settle in and resume my life. Some friends and family asked me if there was any chance for reconciliation. My response was, "Not in this lifetime and not on this planet." I was angry at Matt and myself for ending up in this familiar predicament. I didn't think that divorce was warranted. I didn't know why Matt was unhappy since all I was doing was anything and everything to make him happy. Nothing made any real sense. Matt couldn't provide examples or indicate what he needed. Before long, I believed he just wanted out. Perhaps, he'd never fully wanted in. Forgiveness didn't seem possible. And then, five months later, something resembling a miracle happened. I forgave Matt. *Or so I thought.*

While living on my own, I delved deeply into learning everything I could about forgiveness and its benefits. I was open to the perspective that everything happens for a reason, challenges are growth experiences, there's good in everything, and opening the heart to love and compassion heals. For a long time, I hovered over cloud nine and vowed I'd found peace at last. But it took some convincing to really believe I'd had a breakthrough. Something was still *off*. I decided that as much as I loved my new perspective, I didn't believe in it one hundred percent. A part of me still wasn't on board. Even so, I did what I usually did. I convinced myself that the process takes time, and that all would fall into place.

Next, I became obsessed with forgiving others to the point where believing that holding onto anything negative was destroying my life. My mission was to become positive and grateful. I became skilled at finding the good in everything and there were times it felt intoxicating; better than alcohol or any drug I'd ever tried. Its effects lasted far longer, too, and I felt *superior* as a person who was so willing and flexible to do whatever it takes to reach a place of peace and harmony by being *so forgiving.*

While I was floating happily above the clouds, I did the unthinkable. I reached out to Matt and apologized for what I thought was my part in things. I was even willing to take the blame he directed my way. I, alone, took on the responsibility for the demise of our relationship. *Do I want to be right or do I want harmony?* I told Matt that I had forgiven him. I also felt a compelling urge to win him back. Deep down, I think I believed he was the only man on earth, at least at that time, that could deem me *lovable.*

Shortly after some emails and phone calls, we met for dinner and began seeing each other regularly. By now, I had become more accommodating than ever before. I didn't realize how I was offending myself by going back into a relationship that was hurtful. My new forgiveness mission had me become what I thought was an exceptional woman, full of love, who craved harmony. We decided to give our marriage another go at it. We were still legally married and planned on finding a home together once our respective leases were up, some eight months later.

During the next two years, several things happened that had a significant impact on my life. My father suddenly passed away; Matt and I purchased a home; I was reinventing my coaching practice; we hired a marriage counselor to help smooth out the rough edges; my mother was reaching her mid-eighties when she got into a minor fender-bender and was told to stop driving; and I made the decision six months into our marriage counseling sessions to stop going. I didn't feel harmony was the goal, and I felt our marriage was breaking apart. I made the commitment to take things into my own hands and become an even more devoted wife and make my marriage work. For four months after leaving therapy, our marriage was the best it ever was, even better than when we were dating. We were respectful of one another, affectionate, having fun, and working hard. *At least in my eyes.*

Then, during a weekend away to celebrate Matt's birthday, we had dinner with another couple at the resort we were staying at. I overheard Matt telling the stranger we met earlier that day that he wasn't happy and that we had nothing in common. "She doesn't ski; she doesn't like sports; she doesn't this; she doesn't that."

Later, I confronted Matt. He let me know that he wasn't happy, even though all the evidence indicated to me that we were doing great. When I asked why or for specific examples, he couldn't offer me any other than we didn't have a lot in common. When we returned home, he insisted we go back to the marriage counselor. Our past visits were stressful and produced arguments clearly provoked by the sessions. So, I didn't see going back to something that was so unproductive as a good solution. I said, "No."

"I don't want to stay in this marriage unless we go back into therapy," Matt said.

"Okay," I said. "I'm not going back."

I never saw it coming. Our friends were surprised, too. I realized later that Matt never really wanted in, which was what I'd suspected after the first go-around. He never had more than one day a week to spend with me, which usually consisted of me tagging along while he ran his weekly errands. Errands would be followed by an unrelaxing dinner that lasted under an hour, and then home to watch *his* TV shows together. All the other times, we spent working. I'm not suggesting that I'm blameless in the demise of my relationship, but my biggest mistake was my willingness to stay in a "marriage in name only" and convince myself I was happy. I believe Matt's attempt to get me back into marriage counseling was a ploy to quickly end the marriage without having to take responsibility for ending our relationship.

We both hired lawyers and started the inevitable process of ending things for good. By now, I was even more confused and conflicted, since I believed I had become a better version of myself. I was a kinder woman, a more devoted wife, a more loving *forgiver*. I was flexible, accommodating, and agreeable. I accepted Matt's inability to give our relationship more quality time, and I became more independent to overcompensate for him calling the shots. Now, I felt angry, cheated, and more abandoned than I'd felt in any of my other relationships. In addition, Matt told me that the life coach we were both talking to individually was more than aware of our two opposing positions. I'd share that we were very happy, and Matt would declare that he was miserable. Matt told me that he gave the coach permission to share his discord with me and was secretly hoping that she would. Not only did she never mention it to me, but, instead, praised me for my efforts and let me know she was happy for me.

When I ended my relationship with the coach, I felt even more abandoned, unsafe, and betrayed. I became guarded and unwilling to trust anyone so easily. In the years to come, I was able to see clearly how I gave professionals the benefit of the doubt because I assumed they were, in fact, *professional.*

As I sat in my office and contemplated how to approach my divorce, I weighed the options in my mind. I intended to be fair and rational while fighting for my rights, something I hadn't done in my previous breakups. This time, I wasn't about to leave with my tail between my legs, a defeated victim accepting an unfair settlement. I chose a path that required me to set boundaries and implement consequences. I had a chance to flex these new muscles after Matt went back on a settlement agreement we'd discussed and agreed was fair. After Matt's lawyer sought to muddy the waters with Matt's permission, I told Matt, "Deal's off!" I then encouraged my lawyer to start playing their game. When it was all over, I got everything I was entitled to. I realized this experience was exactly what I needed to live my life on higher ground. I couldn't have suspected it then, but this event sparked my profound healing. I was finally focusing on me.

But being a People Pleaser was wreaking havoc in my life. My newfound spiritual teachings, especially those about forgiveness, pushed my People Pleasing behavior to a destructive high. I became less responsible for myself and more responsible for everyone else's bad behavior. I rewarded their offenses while demeaning myself. It now made sense that my relationships were strained. I now had the missing piece to the mystery puzzle that had me scratching my head for decades. Things were now making perfect sense. In addition to doing everything to make others happy while neglecting my own needs and desires, I believed it wasn't acceptable to have a mean bone in my body or to dislike anyone. But deep down, my hatred for people who'd wronged me was always there. I'd come to distrust and blame those people while loathing myself more in the process. If my relationship with Matt hadn't opened my eyes, I might still be living the lie I lived for years. It was now time to tweak my perspective on forgiveness and tailor it to be the right fit for me.

Today, I hold a new perspective on forgiveness that weaves several important rules I follow to support how I forgive. These work well for me. While making myself my first priority, and fully owning my self-expression, my rules for forgiveness don't let anyone off the hook. They also allow my mind to remain peaceful and free from rumination. It has remarkably reduced my resentment toward others and certainly played a huge part in forgiving my mother. In fact, it was because of my desire to better my relationship and forgive my mother that my rules of forgiveness came to be.

My rules of forgiveness are empowering to the self, fair and loving to others, and helps to create authentic, mutually respectful relationships. I consider it a loving practice for how I view the world while, at the same time, validating my feelings without making anything wrong. This liberates me to express myself in a radically honest way with myself and to make choices and decisions that are in my best interest. I consider this the most loving choice because we can't be authentic with others if we're not honest with ourselves. Even when we choose to end relationships with people who want to stay in our lives, it's the best decision for them as well, if staying means we're not being true to them either. Lying to ourselves deceives others as much as it betrays ourselves.

To become the best version of ourselves, we must practice integrity and that requires we get to our truth, whatever that looks like. We won't like everything we find, but we will feel the wholeness of what it is to be human. Once we summon the love for ourselves, we become eligible to connect with others in a healthy way.

These rules are in no particular order. I've numbered them here for organization purposes. For me, personally, each rule must be incorporated, for me to find peace and resolution within my mind and heart. I suggest you consider each one carefully and take what feels right while putting aside the rest. Remember, there is no *one size fits all* when it comes to the way we see things. There are many different perspectives. We must choose the one that feels right for us. I must happily admit that, so far, the people I've shared my rules for forgiveness with are doing the happy dance and are experiencing a better relationship with themselves and others.

FORGIVENESS RULES:

RULE #1: Forgiveness is about letting go, not giving in: Don't reward bad behavior! There's nothing worse than being offended and then feeling like a fool when rewarding your offender's bad behavior. This is a time to withhold, not to give. Withholding includes your time, attention, compassion, and communication. If your offender is someone you don't live with, avoid all contact with them until you've processed your feelings around what's happened and how you want to handle it. You don't owe them any explanations. The less you say, the better, and you don't have to say anything at all. No words speak the loudest.

RULE #2: Feel how you truly feel, not how you think you should feel: Stop glossing over your dark thoughts just to be more positive or to avoid feeling the pain. You've just been offended or even betrayed. Feel how you feel. If you're angry, sad, frustrated, or humiliated, feel it. Feel, feel, feel. Anything you feel will pass through you. Anything you suppress will grow and fester. As hard as it may be, I also encourage to not talk to friends about what happened. As well-intentioned as friends are, their opinions aren't as important as yours. Sometimes, they can sway the way you feel and steer you in directions you don't feel comfortable going in. Also, chiming in about your offender, as good as this may feel, will only intensify and prolong the time you need to get past what happened. Sharing with a professional is a better choice since they can help you get to your feelings, instead of rehashing the details and how *others* feel about what's happened. This is a fertile time to learn about yourself and support your healing and growth. Don't miss out on this opportunity. It's also a great time to channel your feelings once you feel them. Kick and scream for a while. If you're sad, cry. Don't fight the tears. If you're angry, beat a pillow, scream in your car, dance to hard rock. Feel, feel, feel! You can't forgive what you're unaware of, what you don't acknowledge, and what's left unprocessed. Pushing things aside to feel good in the moment won't last over time.

RULE #3: Don't make excuses for your offender: Don't justify and rationalize why your offender did what they did. Don't go into the story about how they had a bad childhood, were overworked and burned out, were drunk, or weren't thinking. You were offended! Don't forget it!

RULE #4: Own that you were victimized: Understand, profess, and embrace that you were violated, offended, and betrayed. Don't minimize it, don't rationalize it, don't deny it, and don't forget it. You can't change anything you don't acknowledge, and you can't forgive what you don't acknowledge. The victim can't become the victor without recognizing the victimization in the first place.

RULE #5: Don't forgive the transgression: Transgressions are not meant to be forgotten or condoned. No one is meant to be relieved of their responsibility in doing what they did. That's why so many people struggle with forgiveness. They're asked to forgive the unforgivable. Transgressions aren't what we forgive. We forgive the people who commit them. Once you understand this, you won't need to keep replaying the events over in your mind, trying to make sense as to why people do what they do. There's no rhyme or reason many times other than the wounding and fear that plague us all. No answers will feel right when someone you love is murdered. No explanation will suffice when your husband or wife runs off with your best friend. Forgiveness isn't meant to excuse anything. Instead, it's designed to release us from the cruel offenses of others so that we can survive and thrive after trauma.

RULE #6: Don't assume you know people intimately because you've been intimate with them: Understand that we all have a dark side. This includes *you*. To live freely, and to experience our wholeness and have self-acceptance and compassion for others, we must understand that we're made up of a complex compilation of all the qualities in the world. We must recognize that we're capable of committing transgressions, including unthinkable ones. We must be aware of this. This doesn't excuse our accountability for the things we do. We are individually responsible for our own behavior.

RULE #7: Don't give anyone the benefit of the doubt: Don't expect your offenders to apologize, change, or make up for their bad behavior. Know instead what they're capable of, and believe them when they show you who they are. For the betrayers that remain in your life, as well as those you dismiss from your life, know that trust is earned, and it must be earned through *actions*, not *words*. Trust what you see, *not* what you *want* to see.

RULE #8: Loss is inevitable: No matter how hard we try to hold on to something or someone to produce the outcome we want, it's inevitable that there will be heartache and loss in our lives. We don't have the power to *fix* or change people. And we certainly have no control over how others think, feel, or behave. It serves no purpose to hold on to that which doesn't feel good or right. Loss can't be avoided.

RULE #9: Not every loss is a loss: Grieving is a necessary step in moving on. But recognize that many offenses happen to better your life. If I use my example with Brad's lies and deceptions that led to our divorce, I can say with conviction that the end of that relationship was the best thing that could have happened for my life. In my relationship with Matt, I discovered my People Pleasing ways and how that behavior needed to stop. Neither of my relationships with these partners was healthy. Know what you're grieving and recognize that sometimes, what you think you have, wasn't in your possession at all.

RULE #10: Don't tell your offender you've forgiven them: For Pete's sake, it's not necessary that your offender know you forgive them. It drives me crazy when I see people in the media declaring they've forgiven the perpetrator that murdered their loved one and either sent them a letter letting them know or declared it in open court! Are you kidding me?

I once saw a Dateline episode where a group of women were discussing the brutal murder of their good friend, Sara. Sara was kidnapped, raped, and murdered in such a violent fashion that the perpetrator cut off her head and mutilated her to hide her identity.

"I know Sara would want me to forgive him," said one of the women. She was smiling and was certain that Sara wouldn't want her to be angry or sad and that it was important to let this man know he was forgiven.

NEWS FLASH: Don't be so sure how your friend would feel! Don't speak for your friends! For any of my friends who are reading this now. If, God forbid, I meet such a demise, I'd want you to be happy and remember all our good times. Please, please, whatever you do, do not tell my perpetrator you've forgiven him! You will have betrayed me!

I'm not surprised so many people struggle with forgiveness. If someone has betrayed you, you don't have to share your insights, and I suggest you don't. Why give them resolution? They don't deserve it from you. Let God bestow forgiveness, not you. It's not your job. Concern yourself with living well and moving on from the transgression. Let these people wonder. It's the only way they'll learn. People who want to be in your life who don't know where they stand will have to do their best to become a standup person. This is where you'll know who belongs in your life and who must go.

In my opinion, telling someone you've forgiven them destroys accountability, excuses the transgression, and diminishes the forgiver's right to have their dark feelings about the offender. I further believe it contradicts all the struggle and processing that leads us to be willing to forgive. Forgiveness is *for giving* to ourselves, not to them. And in the same way, we shouldn't expect others to tell us, either. We must hold ourselves accountable for our transgressions and make the choice to become better people. We deserve the opportunity to learn and heed our lessons, too.

RULE #11: We can dislike others and still love humanity: We can dislike other people and still have an open heart to love. We can forgive someone that we dislike. We can have compassion for someone we dislike. What's important is to get real with our feelings. I have forgiven many people in my life. Many I remain fond of even though I've not stayed in contact. There are a select few who I don't like at all. Even so, I appreciate and exercise my love for humanity, choosing to believe that most people have good within them.

RULE #12: Find your compassion and energetically deliver it: Just as all humans have a dark side, we each have a light side, too. Everyone was born with innocence and the essence of love. It's what happens in our lives that changes who we are. Fear cuts us off from our loving essence. To free our minds from brooding on betrayals and evil acts, it's helpful to imagine our offender as an innocent child before the *damage* was done. In this way, we can send compassion not to who the offender is now, but to the *soul* of the innocent. This will allow us to forgive the innocent and not the guilty.

RULE #13: You must forgive yourself for everything: Because you'll be the only person who's fully present from the moment of your birth, your death, and each moment in between, you must hold unconditional love and forgiveness for the self. It's the only way you'll be able to move on and become a better person. You, too, were once an innocent. All of us must love ourselves without condition, not to permit ourselves to be bad and offensive, but instead to find the opportunity to reclaim our love essence. Self-forgiveness is the most powerful form of forgiveness because our judgment is what drives our behavior.

RULE #14: Make your mission more important than your misery:
Even the worst tragedies in life can be used as leverage to create a better life. All that's needed is the willingness to use the bad for the good. My favorite example of this is the incredible story of John Walsh, whose six-year-old son, Adam, was abducted from a Florida Mall and murdered in 1981. Later, John and his wife, Reve, created The National Center for Exploited and Missing Children and later, TV's *America's Most Wanted* with John Walsh as the host. The show was responsible for apprehending numerous criminals and bringing them to justice.

RULE #15: Everything that happens is leverage for creating an extraordinary life: As George Herbert once said, "Living well is the best revenge."

Live your life to the fullest. Claim what you deserve! And don't let anyone take away your joy. I believe if we've lived through a lot of bad, we deserve a lot of good to make up for it. It's all available and attainable. After we weep, we must reap.

STEP SEVEN: CONSIDER THE BENEFITS OF FORGIVENESS AND FIND THE WILLINGNESS WITHIN YOU.

The biggest intention of this book is for you to find joy in your life. Forgiving your mother and yourself are essential to attaining the life you desire. Forgiveness will help to spark your desire to claim what you deserve. I believe that desire is *bigger* than fear.

Take some quiet time to journal your feelings about forgiveness and allow yourself to recognize that you are the benefactor in this transaction. I like to play with the word *forgiveness* a bit as it helps me to see more clearly. Break down the first two syllables, *for* and then *give,* and imagine these sentences: *For* them, I *give* myself the gift of claiming what I deserve in life, despite what they've done to harm me. I'm entitled to joy and happiness, and no one will stop me from claiming it.

Be kind and compassionate as you reflect on forgiveness. You're now on step seven, which means you're well on your way to forgiving your mother.

Chapter 8

REOPENING YOUR EYES

Our eyes see what our mind believes.

"I'm sorry you see things that way."

Ever fall prey to self-doubt or feel crazy when others convince you that you're just plain wrong in the way you see things?

There's no greater struggle than believing that you're wrong, that everyone else is right, and that your reality is blurred by the way you look at the world. I've felt that way most of my life. Today, I know for certain that everything I saw and the way I saw it was one hundred percent accurate. It always was. It always is. And it always will be.

When it comes down to how we see ourselves, others, and the world, all that matters is the way *we* perceive and integrate *our* experiences. In every relationship we participate in, all that counts is how *we* internalize *our* perception of things. What *we* see and what *we* overlook seeing is all that's important because it's *our* reality. I'm certain that we're accurate in what we see based on the meaning we give to it. I'm further certain that everyone else is right, too, because it's how *they* evaluate what *they* see. And I'm convinced that how *we* see things is based on how *our* minds manipulate our eyes through conditioning, programming, and experiences we've lived through. *What you see is what you believe* is as accurate as *What you believe is what you see.*

When we're not encouraged to express ourselves when we're young and don't get the acknowledgment for how we think and behave, then we learn very early to doubt how we see things and the ways we feel about things. No one likes to feel crazy. As much as we struggle for autonomy and validation—yearning to matter and to be loved and accepted in the world—unless we're guided to look within and love ourselves, we'll be at the mercy of others to show us how to see.

Our childhood is the most impressionable time of our lives. It's when our wonder and curiosity are at their peaks. The learning we experience is essential for our growth and understanding of how the world works and what it means for us. It's also the time we're trapped in whatever predicaments our caretakers create for us, as well as when we make our decisions about who we are and what we're capable of. If we're not nourished and nurtured, if we don't have the assurances we need to make us feel safe, protected, and loved; fear will prevail. So, for most of us, when things happen that go against our need for security, we rationalize, justify, and gloss over what we're seeing to avoid the discomfort. We begin living a lie.

I don't remember a lot about my early years as a child, and yet I have some vivid glimpses into memories that have never left me. I remember sitting up in bed at four years old recovering from a tonsillectomy. The room was very white, and I remember the cold metal bars surrounding my bed. My father was feeding me ice cream, and my throat was very sore. I remember vomiting. I also remember needing my mother and her not being there.

At five, I woke up in the middle of the night screaming. My father turned on all the lights. "See honey, there are no spiders here. Nothing is crawling all over you." There was no calming me down. I saw what I saw. I felt what I felt. I remember needing my mother and her not being there.

I remember the blood running down my face and onto my favorite party dress on our way to a birthday celebration. My sister was there. My mother was driving. I can feel the pain of the needle as the doctor stitched me up and the force of the nurse's hands as she held me down on the table covered in dark green vinyl. I can see the yellow foam where there was a large tear in the cushion. I can still taste the saltiness as my tears mixed with the cherry-flavored lollipop I got when it was all over. I remember the nurse saying, "You're such a brave girl." She smiled widely, and her teeth were pretty and white. I don't remember my mother comforting me. I was six years old. I remember needing her.

I recall the time I was showing off in front of my friend and her sixteen-year-old brother when I did a handstand against the wall in their basement. My friend suddenly grabbed me and pulled me off into the bathroom. "You're bleeding!" she said. "I think you got your period! You should go home and tell your mother." I was eleven years old, and I was terrified. I had no idea what my friend was talking about or what any of it meant. I thought I was dying. I remember my mother wasn't home. My grandmother helped me. I don't remember my mother comforting me. She spent the night on the phone calling everyone with the news. I was horrified and alone.

When I became a young teenager and started high school, I remember asking my mother a lot of questions. I distinctly remember needing her guidance and feeling confused about what to do about boys, how to get through my homework, and who should become my friends. My strongest memories were the times she waited up for me when I became sixteen, started dating and was permitted to go to parties. I had a curfew of 11:00 p.m. When I returned home, she'd ask if I had a nice time and then head off to bed.

As I grew older, I began feeling more compassion for my father. I had blamed him for being mean to my mother, but the more I got to know and experience her, I grew to understand that my father didn't have it easy, either. I found my mother to be unsupportive and discouraging. If you had a parade going on, she'd find a way to rain on it. I was beginning to see the real dynamic in my parent's marriage. It was around this time that my resentment grew for my mother.

Along with the challenges of becoming a teenager, fitting in, and striving to be popular, I felt embarrassed and ashamed of my parents and their weird ways of relating. At the same time, I was still desperately trying to please them. I felt particularly anxious when introducing them to a boy I was dating. Looking back, I see how I was trying to manage other people's behavior. I tried to control all interactions, believing I had the power to do so. I believed that I was the catalyst for change. I took things personally as if everything was my fault or everything was fixed by me. When things went my way, I'd beam with pride. When things didn't go my way or someone became disappointed or angry, my world was shaken to the core.

Along with the lack of guidance or encouragement in shaping who their children would grow up to be in the world, my parents insisted that my sister and I surround ourselves with Jewish friends, particularly the people we chose to date. But that request was similar to their other ways of childrearing. Enforce the rules without a guidebook.

My parents weren't very observant Jews. They did enroll us in Hebrew school, but we only went for two years. They did host dinners on the Jewish holidays, but didn't follow the traditions that they made fun of. My sister and I didn't gain an understanding of what it means to be and live as a Jew. What we did see was anger and resentment of other ways of living. It was this negative judgment toward others that turned me off. For young children, when such demands aren't supported with compassion and good reason, they create more resistance than desire. It was predictable we'd rebel. And, even though I later married three times, each to a Jewish man, it was more out of my need to feel familiar and safe than it was to follow my parents' rules, even though selecting Jewish men did earn me points in their eyes.

What strikes me most as I recall these times in my life, is that I had no clue that my mind and my judgments were running the show.

Even today, I can see how my relationship with my parents, husbands, friends, and coworkers contributed to the dysfunction I experienced. But back then, I was pointing the finger, and I was certain I knew it all.

Now that you're walking steadily toward forgiveness, it's imperative to recognize that your perspective, true and accurate, is limited, and that a shift in perception may change everything you previously believed. I liken it to reading a book or watching a movie for the second or third time. Things you missed the first time around are now obvious and explain things in a different way. If you're willing to open your mind to look for the benefits in things instead of highlighting the challenges, you'll bring about a positive change in your life and relationships. Everything depends on what you're thinking.

Remember we discussed how you and your mother each have your own *story?* The great thing about our stories is that we can tweak them at any time by choosing to see things differently. All it takes is willingness and the desire to find light in the dark.

I experience shifts all the time these days. And I marvel at how much control I really do have when it comes to attracting what I *want* to see. It's not that the world has changed; I've changed the way I think and choose to look at things. I'm doing the happy dance a lot these days because of it.

Several years ago, I allowed myself to trust my intuition with great success. I suddenly had a new perspective on myself, my parents, and the world. It sent me into an emotional release that cut loose the heavy burdens I'd carried for years, and it unleashed my joy for who I am and what I represent. I understood that I'd misjudged my mother and lost precious bonding time with her. At the same time, I gave myself some grace for having seen things the way I did and recognized that I wasn't *wrong;* instead, I was *thinking and seeing* in the dark.

"Watch the movie, The Diary of Anne Frank!

It was the third time my mind screamed the request. I was participating in an internal visualization exercise led by the life coach I hired to support me to move through some challenges. Each of our sessions had required homework including action steps that arose through the meditation. I heard it loud and clear.

I've seen the movie. I read the book. I know the story. I contemplated whether this action step was a waste of time. *What's there to discover in something I already know?* Once things unfolded, I would no longer have the need to ask myself that question, not ever again. This time though, I chalked it up to Patricia Heller's quote, "If you hear the message three times, listen." So, I went online and ordered a remake of the movie, *The Diary of Anne Frank*. Three days later, the DVD arrived, and I scheduled time on Saturday morning to watch it by myself without distraction.

I was crying uncontrollably by the end of the movie. The movie sparked an epiphany about myself, my family, and the Jewish people that rocked me to my core.

For many years, I couldn't fathom how over six million Jews died during this atrocity. I hadn't read much about this time in our history, my parents didn't share much, and aside from some movies such as *Schindler's List*, *The Pianist*, and *The Reader*, I wasn't well informed. But given what I knew from my parents and their friends who survived World War II as well as what I learned in school, I wondered why the Jews didn't put up more of a fight?

As a young girl, I saw my parents cower in situations where their voice needed to be heard. I saw their friends go silent and act insecure. Somewhere, I decided they were like this because they were weak. I felt uneasy and uncomfortable in their company because they focused on the persecution they'd survived. This narrative didn't fit in with my desires. I wanted to be popular and loved. I couldn't believe that nobody attempted to change the fate of the Jews. I just knew I'd have done anything to fight back, even if it meant being riddled by bullets and losing my life. I judged them as cowardly.

Now, after watching *The Diary of Anne Frank* at this junction in my life and development, I realized that it wasn't weakness that these people embodied, but instead the incredible will to live. The Jews were made to suffer in unthinkable ways, and yet it was their strength, resiliency, belief in their values, and the desire to hold on to life that allowed so many to survive. Tears are forming even as I write this. I feel so much love and compassion for my parents, myself, and everyone who was affected by this tragedy. And, even though I consider myself spiritual and not religious, I am prouder than ever to be a Jew.

I experienced a shift of enormous magnitude. It taught me that as much as I can change my mind, and often do, I, too, can change my perspective. All I must do is choose to open my mind and allow myself to see with fresh eyes.

Now it's time for you to take another important step forward.

STEP EIGHT: CHOOSE TO SEE DIFFERENTLY.

Take this time to give yourself the opportunity to bring hope and faith into your life and allow yourself to see things in new ways. Recognize that what you're thinking about you're bringing about. Your thoughts, beliefs, judgments, etc., are affecting your experiences, your relationships, and your state of mind.

Think of a time in your life where you had a change of heart or once saw things from one perspective and then another. It's good to remember these experiences because they help us to recall that we can see things in various ways.

When you think about your mother, write down some judgments you have about her and then ask for the willingness to open your eyes and see her differently. Do you judge her harshly? Does she push your buttons without even opening her mouth? Now is the time to start creating some shifts in the way you see things, because whether you know it or not, or like it or not, you and she are intertwined.

Be kind and compassionate with yourself. This isn't about making anyone right or anyone wrong. This is about choosing to see things from a perspective that lights you up and brings you peace.

Breathe deeply. Close your eyes and imagine a scenario. Then imagine various ways you can interpret that scenario. Find a way that feels good and make sure it makes sense. We're not aiming to gloss over anything; we're looking for a fresh way to see.

Chapter 9

THINK BEFORE YOU ACT AND WALK LIGHTLY

Walking on eggshells can teach us respect.

Now that you've made it this far in the book, whether you've taken the recommended steps or chosen to read them for now and give them some thought, it's imperative to understand that any change, any shift in mindset, will impact the status quo in your relationship with your mother.

When we're carrying resentment for someone, we may display behavior that's either hostile and combative or that contradicts how we're really feeling, and it's inauthentic. I'm going to highlight the latter, since I believe it's even more destructive than the former. Being hostile and combative with someone you resent makes sense. But when we pretend to be nice, People Please, pretend, or deceive while holding resentment, we attract the most toxicity into our lives. I've found that being phony and superficial covers up our true feelings and will, at some point, backfire big time.

I am a firm believer that honesty isn't the best policy when the communicator isn't skilled at communicating. When we're holding onto resentment, we're not equipped to get our point across in a way that's respectful to anyone, including ourselves. Furthermore, if we've been inauthentic in the relationship all along, which means our feelings and actions are at odds with each other, we behave in ways that give others the impression that we're fine when we aren't. Then, we're the ones living the lie. Eventually, we'll explode or implode and attack the person we pretended to be nice to. Our inauthenticity will be exposed and have others thinking that we're crazy, phony, and even dangerous to be around. The greater tragedy is when we don't recognize our behavior and we continue to sabotage our relationships and push love away. This happens often with People Pleasers. They're so invested in being liked and worried about what people think of them that they can't see they're the common denominator in their relationships. If this sounds confusing, the next story should clear it up.

Wait. What? Did I just read that? Did I just receive this from Ruth?

I was doing some work at my computer when the text chimed in on my phone. I couldn't believe what I was reading.

One month ago, I met Ruth for lunch at a local restaurant close to where we both live. It was right around the holidays, and everyone was in a good mood. We exchanged small gifts. I gave her a paperweight that highlighted a special quote by Emily Dickinson, "Forever is composed of nows." I was thankful for the pretty pink journal Ruth had given me.

During lunch, Ruth shared some challenges she was going through with her daughter and asked me for advice. I validated her perspective with, "I can understand how you feel hurt and why this is challenging for you." When she kept pressing me for what to do or how to approach this or that, I gave her *my* opinion of what *I* would do.

Our conversation flowed nicely, and Ruth then asked me if I see anything in her behavior that may be concerning that could explain her daughter's resentment toward her. She said she valued my opinion and speaking to a seasoned coach may shed some light on what she isn't seeing. I told Ruth that without the full story and not knowing how her daughter is feeling, I could only give my best hypothesis. After asking Ruth if she was willing to hear about a pattern I was picking up on, that may be responsible for her strained relationships, she answered with an emphatic, "Yes!" She was smiling and eager to hear what I had to say.

"I have a strong sense that what you're feeling and the way you're behaving is inconsistent and at odds. You say you want one thing, yet you go about it as if you want another. Mixed messages are flying about, and your daughter is most likely confused. It may be helpful if you figure out what you really want and stop looking to her to figure it out."

"Wow, that's interesting." Ruth said. "I never thought about it that way. Thanks. That was really helpful."

After eating our delicious lunch, we parted with smiles and hugs and went our separate ways.

We may have communicated by a text or two with wishes for a "Happy New Year" or a quick question about a restaurant, but it wasn't unusual for us to touch base infrequently. We enjoyed each other's company, but our friendship was new and evolving.

So, when I received Ruth's text one month later, I was taken aback and insulted by her message. Voicing what she called her "honest truth," she mentioned that she hoped "it goes over well, as she's not a good communicator." She wrote, "I felt analyzed, judged, and criticized by you." She then went on to explain how angry she was and that I have a part in her "pain."

I responded with an appropriate text explaining how I now felt. I validated Ruth for her feelings; but disagreed with this new offensive behavior toward me. I reminded her that I'm not a mind reader and that she seemed completely engrossed in our conversation and *acted* as if she was thankful for my input. I had a hunch that she experienced some painful thoughts afterwards because I'd provided an accurate assessment of the situation, and she felt uncomfortable. It was also possible that she was upset with herself because she insisted on picking up the check even though I asked her not to. Maybe I hadn't gotten in touch to reciprocate soon enough. Who knows? I didn't exactly know what had set her off, and I wasn't going to give it a lot of thought. In the past, issues like this could send me ruminating for weeks.

I mention this story here, because it's a great example of what I've discussed above. When we behave in a way that contradicts how we feel, the resentment builds. When we desire to now be upfront and honest with others, we end up in a resentment rant because we blame *them* for the crappy way we feel. In the end, we sabotage ourselves.

These days, I find myself forgiving others more readily based on my new set of rules. But one thing that's helped me to love and respect myself more than ever is my trustworthy "no moregiveness" rule. When someone has offended me, for whatever reason and where I've not provoked it, I choose to *give no more* to them, if and unless they earn back my good graces. If it's someone like Ruth who isn't someone close to me, I dismiss them from my life. I believe we're two good women who exchanged a mutual lesson for growth. The loss will help it marinate. For others who are close and intimate such as my mother, other family, coworkers, or long-time friends, I take a step back and watch future behavior. But more importantly, I stay true to my perspective while considering others. What makes the most sense for me and what protects me from toxic energy is what I choose for my life today. At sixty-one, I'd rather move on than stay in a relationship that makes me angry at me.

I'll also think carefully about what I say to others, how I say it, and be compassionate and respectful to the people who deserve this from me. I'm careful when communicating my disappointment with others and make it a practice to not point my finger and use the word, "You," at the beginning of a confrontation. It's attacking and accusatory, and it disregards one's own responsibility for owning feelings. As Eleanor Roosevelt once said, "No one can make you feel inferior without your consent."

As I embarked on my path to forgive my mother, after having gone through the last eight steps, I was now ready to examine my behavior and how I was using communication in my relationship with my mother.

When we choose to tell ourselves the truth and not make anything wrong about who we are and the ugly things we find, we liberate ourselves in ways we can't imagine. As Carl Jung once said, "I'd rather be whole than good." As Debbie Ford once said, "The gold is in the dark."

It was my turn to face the mirror and own that I was responsible for the strained relationship with my mother. It was me who was making her the *burden* in my life instead of the *blessing*. I had found the answer to healing myself. It was time to begin creating the extraordinary life I was missing out on.

STEP NINE: EXAMINE THE BEHAVIOR AND WAYS OF COMMUNICATION YOU'RE USING IN YOUR RELATIONSHIP WITH YOUR MOTHER.

Out of all the steps, this one requires the most patience and willingness because it can feel offensive to those of us who feel overly victimized and blame ourselves for everything. If you're like me and have taken responsibility for others in your life, it may feel self-degrading to point the finger back at you for doing anything wrong. If we're doing everything to make sure everyone is happy, and especially if we're failing at it, how could we take on another task? It's not fair! Right?

The point here is recognizing that in our relationships, we're usually unaware of our own behavior. This is partly because we can't see ourselves and partly because we're focused on how others are treating us. When we're doing things we really don't want to do, and keeping an inventory about them, we start building resentment. To take our power back, we must know what that means and connect with the control we do have. This is where it gets exciting because we all have one hundred percent control over ourselves. Once you embrace that you can attract great relationships and experiences by changing your mindset, you'll be blown away with how life brightens up.

To forgive your mother and yourself, it's going to require that you see what you're doing that's working against you. Even if your mother is so toxic that it's not possible to have a relationship *with* her, you can still have a different relationship in your mind *about* her. Remember, forgiveness is for *you*. This book is about *your* healing. And, it can also be about *her* healing if you're willing to make the first move and be the hero in your family.

Take out your journal and spend some time meditating about the things you do, the things you say, the way you *dance* in your relationship with your mother. This isn't to make you wrong. It's not even to say your behavior isn't warranted. Instead, it's to open your eyes to a different way of thinking and being. Don't lose sight of the gift at the end of all of this. We're aiming for you to get the life you've always wanted. I'm just showing you the way.

Kudos to you! Here's to soaring!

Chapter 10

POWER PLAYS AREN'T POWERFUL

Every relationship needs a hero. Put on your cape.

"Yes! I agree! You're being screwed!"

Whenever my mother was being negative and judgmental, I'd resist her behavior and quickly jump in with solutions: "Why don't you just relax and do it this way?" "Don't be so negative; stop complaining already!" Sometimes, I'd run amok out of frustration in having to fulfill her every need and make her happy. It was exhausting! I was constantly trying to change her behavior. Soon, I realized it wasn't her; it was me. I didn't like being around negative people, and I judged them harshly. In addition, as a People Pleaser, I made it my responsibility to make *them* feel better. I didn't do well in environments that weren't harmonious. I didn't yet recognize that my need to control others and the world was making me defeated and hopeless.

Today, I live my life peacefully by following a practice that brings me serenity while letting go of the self-inflicted burdens I used to carry. In the past, I believed that everything reflected on me. Somehow, some way, I felt responsible for everyone and their bad behavior. If others became sad, got angry, or complained, I'd have to *fix* it and make it better. And, I couldn't rest until I'd tried everything. It was exhausting! That's what it feels like to reach for power we don't have. We can't control other people.

Then, out one day with my mother, while she was being her normal, negative, judgmental self and going on about this or that, I chimed in. Instead of fighting her, resisting her bad energy, or finding ways to make her feel better, I did something I hadn't tried before. I agreed with her. Now mind you, I was frustrated. I wasn't testing out a new technique, I just got tired of defending my position and changing the dynamic. So, I became an echo for her instead. I reflected back everything she said and then took it a step further by validating her.

"Yes," I said. "They're wrong; you're right." "That's totally unfair." "You're kidding me, they said that?" "How awful!" I chimed in with everything and took her side. I wasn't being sarcastic. I was joining her crusade. And guess what? After a moment or two, she stopped. There was a moment or two of silence and then she changed the subject. She smiled and asked me some questions about what was going on in my life. I almost fell off my seat. *Wow, I think I'm on to something here.*

When I returned home later, I thought about what a nice time I'd had with my mother and realized that just like me, my mother wanted to be heard. All her negativity, complaints, and judgments were all a cry to be heard. So many people are suffering because they feel misunderstood and hopeless. The new rage toward positivity has made complaining and venting a no-no. We forget that we need validation to assuage our self-doubt, especially if we're insecure and not supportive of ourselves.

I found it more productive to listen and validate my mother instead of trying to cheer her up and change who she is. We want to protect our precious energy at all costs, but if we make the choice to lend an ear without having to dream up solutions and strategies to solve people's problems for them, we won't have to exert our effort and exhaust ourselves. Even if we don't agree with what they're saying, and especially if we see things differently, we don't have to be the savior. A hero will do.

Before I go on, I want to be clear about a few important criteria. I don't want to contradict what I've stressed earlier. You must consider yourself first in any relationship you engage in. If it doesn't feel good to be around certain people or if they're abusing you in any way, my suggestion is to not see them, if they're easily avoidable. For those people you can't so readily get away from or family members whom you desire to have a better relationship with, it pays to approach things strategically. Sometimes, you won't get a desired outcome, but frequently the result is a thumbs-up.

I've successfully changed my relationship with difficult people by holding a different picture in my mind about them. It takes some time, effort, and skill to do this, especially if these people trigger us or we're in the habit of negatively judging them. But once we see them differently in our mind's eye, we can calm down while sending positive energy their way. Specifically, I create a scenario in my imagination where they're happy and doing well. I even visualize them smiling and celebrating. If they're having financial difficulties or are physically ill, I imagine these challenges have worked themselves out, and they're healing. This not only sends loving energy to others, it relieves me of the responsibility to make things better for them, which isn't my responsibility or even in my power to do so. And with strained relationships, seeing those people in a better place will help us to see more objectively and allow us to focus on what the right decision is for us. So often, people stay in bad relationships way too long because they feel guilty or don't want to hurt the other's feelings. Staying isn't loving or empowering to any party involved; in fact, it's disempowering and arrogant. All people have the right to be happy and no one needs anyone else to get there. People tend to hold each other back more than to propel them forward. Self-love is the antidote to insecurity and sabotage. When we imagine people in a good place, we're gifting them a blessing and giving ourselves peace of mind. I like to call it an *active prayer*.

When I chimed in during my mother's negative rant, I felt less stress. It took more energy to negatively judge her, and I was attacking myself. That's why it felt so bad. The more I joined her in her thinking, the less she complained. And even when she did, I wasn't plugged in emotionally anymore. She was the one having a bad day, not me. As I became less judgmental toward my mother, allowing her to speak her mind, she soon started saying the words I'd always wanted to hear. "You're such a great daughter." "I love you so much." "I am so proud of you and who you've become." Each time I saw her, she would light up. And before long, I looked forward to our visits. *Thank you, God. You've answered my prayers. I am feeling love for my mother.*

By the time my mother's dementia kicked in, she was repeating herself incessantly, which became a challenge for me. First, I didn't consider myself to be the most patient of people. Second, as she was losing her mind, I became fearful of losing her. Regardless of our relationship over the years, I took for granted that my mother would always be there, even when I believed she wasn't much of a mother to me. I still needed her. I always clung to the hope that we'd resolve our issues and move on. Fear affects people in different ways. When I'm scared, I can get anxious, frustrated, panicky, and even belligerent. I found myself becoming snippy and intolerant of having to answer the same questions with the same replies over and over and over again. But I knew that my mother would continue her decline and one day die. And I could either accept this new reality or resist it, just like when I chose to chime in with her. I chose acceptance.

I found a way to engage on a deeper level with my mother even though we were talking about things that weren't in present reality. For instance, early in my mother's journey with dementia, she forgot my father had died. She'd ask where he was and why he wasn't home. If I'd ask her what year it was, she might reply 1941 and think she was back in Eastern Europe. So, instead of reminding her of the correct year, I'd ask her details about that year or where she thought she was. During this time, I began to bond with my mother in a way I hadn't before. Again, I joined her. I became the hero. I stopped fighting, resisting, or persisting. I chose to breathe and surrender into where things were at the time and stop manipulating for a specific outcome.

Life got easier.

STEP TEN: STOP RESISTING THINGS YOU CAN'T CONTROL.

If you want to forgive your mother and change your relationship with her, whether to connect with her or just in your imagination, become the hero. Stop resisting her ways of being and end the power plays. They won't produce harmony or happiness.

In any challenge we face in life, willingness is the key to breaking through what ails us. In fact, it's our stubbornness that will keep us in situations that don't feel good. Take a deep breath, put down the boxing gloves, and make the decision to take a step forward. Just like I chimed in with my mother, maybe there's something that comes to mind that you can do when you're with your mother to break the ice or to test the waters with something new that may make her feel you care about her.

Remember, it's not about making anyone right or wrong. Instead, it's about validating her so things can change. Doing this will shift the energy. If you stop resisting and hold a better picture of your mother in your imagination, it's a fair shot that the dynamic may shift. Nothing happens overnight, but nothing ever happens if you don't take a step.

Keep in mind, even if you're met with animosity or joining her seems futile, you can still change the picture in your head. And once you do, there will be change. You'll see.

Be kind and compassionate with yourself. You're a hero, and I salute you.

Chapter 11

THE BIGGEST LIE I EVER TOLD

Make the choice to respect each other not to "get" each other.

"I'm lying here like a latke!"

This was my mother's predictable response to my usual question, "How are you today?" Her answer made me wonder. *Interesting choice of words, likening oneself to a pancake made of grated potato.*

Once my mother's dementia worsened, it was no longer safe for her to live by herself. That's when I hired Elisa, a Jamaican-born woman who was as sweet as pie and strong enough to handle my mother. Sometimes, my mother would wake up in the middle of the night and try to leave her home to go look for my father. One time, she even got up on a chair to reach the top lock. Elisa, who slept with one eye open, was on top of things, and I knew my mother was safe in her care. My mother could become belligerent and hard to manage. I didn't experience these episodes. I learned about them through the stories Elisa told me. They were hard to believe since my mother was such a docile woman.

One day, my mother was taken in an ambulance to the emergency room complaining of chest pain and having difficulty breathing. It was discovered she had a large blood clot in her lung. Her doctor was astonished that she was breathing. She also had bad circulation in her left leg that required surgery to correct. The night my mother was back in her room recovering from surgery earlier that day, she went into a tantrum-like fit where she pulled out her I.V., spit and cursed at the nurses, and tried to get out of bed. I was astonished because I'd never heard my mother use profanity or barely raise her voice. I'd heard of such episodes after anesthesia, and I wasn't worried. You may find this strange and out of character, but I was impressed that my mother had fight left in her. *I knew there was a bitch in there somewhere!* I'd hoped to see my mother stand up for herself all my life. I'd wished she'd modeled that for me. I'm not suggesting that throwing things and yelling profanity is the goal, I'm referring to the fight within us to speak our truth and stand our ground, which can be done with grace. Then again, sometimes kicking and screaming is appropriate. There's a time for everything. Whereas I was sorry for the distress my mother was going through, I was entertaining myself by imagining what had gone on.

When my mother returned home, she spent a lot of time in bed, watching tv, and doing crossword puzzles, which, dementia or not, she was still pretty skilled at. She only got out of bed to use the bathroom or to sit in the dining room that overlooked the ocean to have her meals. She no longer wanted to go to the pool or walk in the lobby. She was depressed. Her "lying here like a latke" comment spoke volumes to me. But each time I suggested a solution or offered activities I could take her to, she resisted.

For years, even before my mother became elderly and ill, I viewed her as lackadaisical and unmotivated. She was bored and would kill the time much in the same way she was doing in her elder years: staying at home, usually in bed watching tv, and sharpening her mind with her word games. In my heart, I believed my mother yearned for more. I knew I wanted more for her. I'd see her light up each time company came to visit. When she was younger and spry, she loved going to cultural events and being around people. My mother craved connection. But just as strong as her desire was to be around others, her fear kept her in the familiar surroundings of her home by herself. I remember when I was growing up that my mother would have a scheduled event to attend that she was excited about. But when the day came, she'd say she wasn't feeling well. I sensed she was faking whatever ailment she used to bow out, and I could see her relief at being released from the obligation. But soon, that feeling of relief would turn into boredom and she'd be miserable again. I wondered about the dialogue that played in her head. Sometimes, I'd go into her room where she'd be tweezing her eyebrow hairs, one by one. With no eyebrows left, she'd have to draw them in with an eyebrow pencil. I knew she was conflicted. But as her daughter, I was too busy judging her to ever "get" what she was all about. *I wonder what makes her tick?*

Two years passed, and my mother was doing well with around-the-clock care. Her building, however, was undergoing one renovation after another. Frequently, certain elevator banks were out of use, sometimes for weeks. My mother's apartment was on the fourteenth floor and disabled elevators made it difficult for Elisa and my mother to get out easily. The building also sat on the beach and was in a mandatory hurricane evacuation zone. Since hurricane seasons last for six months and the building renovations seemed endless, I knew I was going to have to move my mother somewhere else. My mother loved looking at the ocean, and I was conflicted about what to do. I knew that if there was a fire or emergency, Elisa would have to get my mother out somehow. But the unreliable elevators meant they'd have to use the stairs. My mother couldn't walk stairs. I knew Elisa was the kind of woman who would stay and die before leaving without my mother, so I had to worry about her, too. It wasn't a safe situation for either of them. It was time to make alternate arrangements.

"Please Mommy and Daddy, I don't want to go. Please let me stay home!"

I was ten years old, and it was a bright sunny day. I got up in the morning and planned to play outside with some friends after breakfast. I had no idea what was happening when my father told me, "We're going for a ride."

I saw my father loading the car from the kitchen window and told my sister, Judy, something was up. "Daddy said we're going for a ride." She looked at me inquisitively, and I shrugged my shoulders back at her.

We all got into the car. My father drove and my mother sat next to him in the passenger seat. Judy and I were in the back. "It's a surprise," my father assured us. Soon, we turned into the shopping mall. I got all excited. *A day of shopping?* My excitement faded as I spotted four enormous buses and lots of people gathered around. My father parked the car, and we got out.

He excitedly told us, "You're going off to sleepaway camp for four weeks! You're both going to have a great time!"

I was a shy, impressionable ten-year-old who felt awkward each time I left my home. There's no way I wanted any part of this. I cried, I screamed, I kicked. And my father put me on the bus. I thought I was going to die, and I didn't want to leave my parents. Judy seemed fine with it, and she put her arm around me. "Don't worry. We're together."

I will never forget that time of my life. I felt afraid and abandoned being left like that to go off to a strange place. If my sister hadn't been with me, I might have passed out. Looking back, what I recall the most was that sleepaway camp gave me some of the best, most memorable years of my life. When my parents came to get us at the four-week mark, which was also "Visiting Day," we begged to stay for the remaining four weeks. They were happy to oblige. We went back for another couple of years.

My parents did something awesome for me, even though I was scared and didn't see it at the time. Now, it was my turn to choose to do something for my mother. Like my father had been, I needed to be strategic in how I pulled it off. *I'm about to tell you the biggest lie I ever told.*

As I was searching for options, I found a wonderful assisted living facility that looked more like an all-inclusive resort. It had beautiful dining rooms, living rooms, libraries, and oodles of activities. They also had a memory care unit where my mother could get the care she needs. Without her knowledge, I put my name on the waiting list and paid a hefty deposit.

I was nervous about making this decision without my mother's knowledge and didn't check in with the facility for months. Part of me was scared because I didn't know how to break the news to my mother. I thought she'd fight me on it. Heck, she didn't even want to stay for a thirty-day trial in a facility when I mentioned moving a year ago. Now, I was just going to take her there? *Remember, camp was some of the best years of my life. Mom will adjust, just like me. She'll love it!*

It was a Wednesday when Julie called me to let me know there was a room now available for my mother. If I want it, I must let them know now and come in with the first month's payment. There were also other obligations I needed to meet, and it would take some time to get all my ducks in a row.

I decorated the room beautifully with furniture from Rooms-To-Go. I used beautiful bedding with fluffy pillows. My mother's basic need, a TV, was placed on the wall in front of her bed. Finally, the day came. Here goes the lie.

I asked Elisa to pack a large suitcase for my mother and herself. I also told her the plan. We'd go for lunch, and afterwards, I'd tell my mother that the building she lives in is closing off the elevators, and she'd be staying in a hotel until the work was done. This wasn't something new, because there were other times we'd had to do this because of the building renovations. I thought my mother would be okay with this arrangement, mainly because she loved staying in hotels.

I was preoccupied at lunch. I could feel the adrenaline coursing through my body. I was picking at my food. I knew that I had to get myself together. I still didn't know how she'd respond. At the very least, I wanted to send good energy and hope that there would be a happy ending. I believed that I was doing the best thing for my mother. I just wasn't sure how right it was. I even thought of my mother as a young teenager having to flee her home and belongings during the war. *Was I evil?* I felt that I was gifting my mother an experience she would enjoy just as she had gifted me with sleepaway camp.

When we entered the facility, my mother exclaimed, "Wow! This place is beautiful. It looks expensive." Then she looked at me and said, "Thank you." I was doing cartwheels in my head. She loved her room and all the people that were making a fuss over her. When I said goodbye to her and Elisa, my mother smiled in a way I'd hadn't seen in years. *God, I love you! Thank you for helping to make this one of the best days of my life!*

I kept her apartment for the next two months before listing it to sell just in case things backfired. I wasn't going to keep my mother anywhere she wasn't happy. And to my immense pleasure, on a visit one day, she called the facility her home and mentioned to me that she remembers once having another home, but she could no longer live there. Wow!

As it turned out, the time my mother spent in her new home was exactly what she needed. She became involved in activities, sang along at shows, and made beautiful artwork. I could hear her gabbing with the other ladies when I visited her in the dining room. She was happy, truly happy. I was happy for her.

I must admit, I still have twinges about lying to get her there. But she was a woman who couldn't receive and was afraid of change. Instead of trying to convince her that she needed to move, I chose to take a risk and do something I believed was a gift for her. And in my case, it turned out magically. You win some, you lose some. This was a blue ribbon.

I chose to hear her cry for help, to recognize that boredom was killing her, and to put my own feelings aside and not let my guilt ruin an opportunity. I was able to make the best decision for her without letting my fear sabotage the opportunity. Both the facility and Elisa's care cost a fortune. It was my mother's fortune to spend, but she wouldn't have spent it on her life, so I made that choice for her. She never believed she deserved much. I felt honored to help her see her worth.

STEP ELEVEN: DON'T TRY TO "GET" HER; RESPECT HER INSTEAD.

Whether you're willing to support your mother or not, be willing to respect her struggle. She's a human being and a woman that's trying to figure things out just like you. Don't try to "get" her and don't expect her to "get" you. I find that when we try to "get" the people we butt heads with, we only hit each other harder and our negative judgment skyrockets. Instead, use that energy with the intention for mutual respect.

Because my mother had dementia, I had to make decisions on her behalf. I aimed to be as respectful as possible, while doing what I believed was in everyone's best interest, especially hers. Her illness made it easier for me to be in charge. It's harder when someone has all their faculties and is resisting you.

Either way, the step here is to find a place in your head and heart where you can respect your mother, agree to disagree, and understand you'll probably not understand each other. You're two unique people with two personal perspectives. Recognize that you're both right and both entitled to your opinions. This makes forgiveness much easier.

Make a simple declaration to yourself that you can write down in your journal. From this moment on, you'll no longer try to figure your mother out. You'll stop trying to understand why she thinks the way she does and why she does the things she does or doesn't do. Free yourself from the burden of finding answers that aren't there. Breathe. Relax. Free your mind.

Chapter 12

PUTTING DOWN THE BATON

It's time to break the cycle and get what you need.

"I'll never be like *her* when I grow up, and I won't treat my children that way."

I remember as a young teenager wanting desperately to win. I was in a hurry to grow up and wanted my freedom to do things my way. I laugh about it now because my parents had been overly lenient. Had I been a mother myself, I would never have considered allowing my offspring the upper hand in the decision-making process. One particular memory stands out.

I had just turned twelve. I was sitting in the dentist office after a cleaning when my mother was called into the room and told that my bite was off. She'd need to schedule an appointment with an orthodontist to see about me wearing braces. I had a few friends at the time who donned their silvery metallic smiles. Candy was called "metal mouth." I thought it was a horrible idea, and I was having no part of it. "I won't cooperate," I told the dentist and my mother. I was thrilled when I got my way. It wasn't until years later that I was pissed off that my teeth were far from perfect. *What kind of mother lets her child decide her healthcare?*

It's common for those of us who've been neglected or abused in childhood to carry on the *bad parenting* and treat ourselves in the same way we were treated by our caretakers. We become conditioned to getting what we believe is what we deserve. Our childhood is our source of reference. We're not only familiar with the level of care, it's as if our parents send us off with a pass of the baton. We grab hold of it and continue the cycle. It's time to put down the baton, end the cycle, and find ways to give ourselves what we didn't get from them.

It's one thing to point a finger at your mother for what she did or didn't do for you in childhood. It's another thing entirely as an adult to blame her and continue to treat yourself badly claiming it's all her fault. This isn't okay, and it won't bring you anything you want. It's a futile attempt to hold her accountable for how badly you feel without owning your responsibility for continuing the cycle.

Years ago, when both my parents were alive, my sister, Judy, and I were visiting them in their Florida home. They lived on the fourteenth floor of a high-rise building. The view was spectacular. All you could see was ocean, as if you were on board a boat in the middle of nowhere. The sand wasn't visible until you walked right up to the glass door and looked down. There was a pool and veranda just off the beach.

My father was playing golf and my mother was in her room. Judy and I were sitting in the living room when she shared a spooky thought that scared her.

"Sometimes," she said, "when I think about my life and our family, I imagine jumping off the terrace just so Mommy and Daddy would feel guilty."

"Oh my gosh!" I responded. "I've had that thought, too!" We began laughing, and I told Judy that they probably wouldn't even *get it*. "They'd probably be stunned and wonder what mental illness we suffered from that they were unaware of." We laughed some more.

Unresolved issues can fester within us, creating more negative experiences and toxic relationships. If we don't deal with our unresolved issues, they'll succeed in convincing us that we're unlovable and unworthy. The good news is that we have one hundred percent control when it comes to how we choose to treat ourselves. It's time to step up our self-care and become a better parent to ourselves.

Each one of us has an inner wounded child who lives within us and who is desperately seeking our attention and love. When we beat ourselves up, make bad choices on our behalf, and feel hopeless that there's any positive change ahead, we re-abuse ourselves. It's unfortunate to be neglected in childhood, but it's even more tragic if we continue treating ourselves badly in adulthood. Negative self-judgment and neglect affect us. The offenses we deal with from others is hurtful, but the beatings we give ourselves are the harshest blows.

I like to imagine that my inner wounded child, whom I refer to as "Evie," using my childhood nickname, who's shy and awkward, is always with me. She reaches for my hand, vying for my attention. Everything that's happening in my life is happening in her life. I've made it my business to consult her on all the decisions I make. "Evie," I say, as I close my eyes and imagine her as a five-year-old in her favorite party dress, "How would you feel if we do this? Do you like so and so? Do you want to have them over for dinner?" When I'm triggered or offended, I sometimes spend way too much time ruminating about the event. With me in a negative spiral, I'm certain Evie feels alone and forgotten. So, to combat the spiral and reengage with her, I remind myself to address my self-care. When I'm unavailable for her, I imagine she goes off to hide in a dark closet. I see myself as her mother, depending on me for everything. Whenever I'm actively engaged with her, I feel my most confident, and I'm less triggered when people push my buttons.

I've also made it a practice, at my wise age of sixty-one years, to move on from offensive people as quickly as I would shoo a fly that lands on my shoulder. My time is precious, and I no longer welcome people who treat me badly. I also believe that people are meant to come and go in our lives. Instead of trying to keep people around who aren't good to us or who don't enhance our lives, or worse, cause us pain, I believe we can forgive people, be thankful for the time we spent together, reap the lessons, and move on. This kind of parting is, more likely than not, mutually beneficial. When I lose my desire to be around someone, I know our connection has run its course. Whatever I may have needed to learn from our connection is complete. It's not loving to spend time with people you don't want to see or be with. It's more hurtful to continue a relationship you don't want to be in than to end a relationship with honesty, dignity, and respect. Sometimes, we don't even have to say anything. The Universe jumps in and parts us. People get busy, the phone stops ringing, and we move on.

On the path to forgiving your mother, learning to love yourself will be crucial to moving forward and thriving. I believe that no one can fill me up or love me in the same way that I can do for myself. Self-love feels like the world is giving me a standing ovation. And there's no greater feeling than when someone doesn't like me, and I feel completely neutral about it. In fact, the less I care about what people think of *me*, the more I care what they think about other things. I become more interested in getting to know people and what they're about because the subject matter is no longer about me.

Self-love plays a role in my relationship and ability to forgive my mother. I've found it helpful to imagine receiving a letter from her that addresses everything I would have liked to hear. Even though I wrote the letter myself, it still has the power to acknowledge that I'm worthy of love and all good things. And it helps to see my mother in my mind's eye in a brighter light.

> *Dear Eve,*
>
> *Words can't express how sorry I am for any hurt I caused you while you were a little girl growing up and even later as an adult.*
>
> *I want you to know there's no excuse for my being hurtful and neglectful toward you. I am your mother, and I was*

responsible for nurturing and protecting you. I am sorry I failed you. I am sorry I wasn't the mother you needed. I wish I'd gotten help for myself. I see that now. I was deeply damaged, which made me incapable of mothering you in the way that you needed and deserved. I had abandoned myself as well.

I want you to know that I'm so proud of you and who you've become, especially despite how insecure and scared you felt most of your life. I'm sad that I didn't encourage and build you up more because you deserved a proud mother. You're a great daughter.

Please forgive me. Your forgiveness means the world to me.

With all my love,

Mom

Reading this letter helped me as I made my decision to forgive my mother and put all my past resentment to bed. It reminded me of what I needed to give myself as I began mothering me. Before my mother had dementia, I brought up some experiences to discuss with her. I had hoped for an apology or for her to take some responsibility, but I was met with confusion and resistance. I was disappointed then, but today, I've come to understand that she couldn't take on any more in her life than the burdens she'd already imposed on herself. Admitting that she wasn't a great mother would have diminished anything she was hanging on to. She was a very unhappy woman. I see that clearly today. The time had come to put down the baton and start a new way of being with me. It was time to make peace with the woman who gave me life. If I'd let her off the hook, I would have been diminishing her potential, which is why I do hold her responsible. But I also release her and love her, knowing that it's now my job to claim my joy.

STEP TWELVE: GIVE YOURSELF WHAT SHE DIDN'T GIVE YOU

I consider this step essential for a happy life. If we'd been taught as children that self-love is the answer to joy and confidence, we wouldn't need therapists or life coaches. There would be more peace in the world, and we'd all shine and reach our potential. Ahh, what a wonderful world that would be.

Write a letter to you that comes from your mother to support you in giving yourself what you didn't get from her. The letter is helpful because it will give you a clear picture of what you need. This isn't designed to bring up resentment for your mother. Remember, you're moving toward forgiveness. Use this exercise to become clear that you are powerful and capable of giving yourself the love that you need. And, if you're willing to delve into another book that I consider one of the best books I've ever read on inner children and self-parenting, I highly recommend *Healing Your Aloneness*, by Erika J. Chopich and Margaret Paul.

Now and always, bring compassion and love as you take this step. Acknowledge yourself for reading this far and considering forgiving your mother. I salute you.

Chapter 13

Last Chapter, Last Day

Look forward, step powerfully, and live your best life.

"T G I F!"

For as long as I can remember, my mother told the same joke every opportunity she got. I must have heard it thousands of times, and it was particularly funny when she told it on a Friday. It went like this:

As a man entered a crowded elevator, he smiled widely at the people inside.

Stepping in to join them, he blurted it out in a loud, cheery voice.

"T G I F!"

Met with collective laughter, a woman in the back yelled out an emphatic: "S H I T!"

Horrified and annoyed, the man looked over his shoulder and glared at her.

"Gosh. Sorry to bother you, lady. I was just saying, Thank Goodness it's Friday."

Equally annoyed the woman replied, "I was just trying to tell you, Sorry, Honey, It's Thursday!"

As God would have it, my mother departed the physical world suddenly on a Friday afternoon. It was the eve of Rosh Hashana, September 7, 2018.

And just like that, Fridays took on a different meaning for me.

Today, as I was writing this last chapter, I realized it's Friday and the seventh day of the month. I don't believe in coincidences. I feel certain that my mother and my father are supporting me in creating this legacy for our family. There may be naysayers who consider it disrespectful to air our dirty laundry, especially since my parents are no longer here to defend themselves. I can assure you that this is told from my perspective only. It's my side of my story, and I wrote it with the intention of supporting forgiveness. I have forgiven both my parents; my father after his death and my mother while she was still very much alive. It has changed my life, and I have faith it has released my parents to heal what they weren't able to while on this planet. I love them both, and I live in honor of them.

It was a Tuesday afternoon, one of the three days of the week that I paid a visit to my mother in the assisted living facility where she lived. When I arrived, it was lunchtime, and I could hear her gabbing with the women in the dining room. My mother's Hungarian accent was obvious, and she spoke louder than she needed to, something I picked up from her. People frequently tell me to "turn it down a notch."

I gave her a hug from behind while Julie, one of the staff members, pulled up a chair so I could join in. My mother beamed when she saw me, "My beautiful daughter, Eve!" she shouted.

My mother never forgot who I was, even though sometimes she'd get confused and talk to me about me as if I wasn't me. I'd have to remind her that she was, in fact, talking to me. "Really?" she'd ask. And then we'd have a good laugh about it.

After lunch was over, I walked my mother to the living room, where we watched some of the women make arts and crafts. That day, my mother had no interest in participating. We spent some time talking and then she said she'd like to lie down. Once in her bedroom, she laid on top of the covers, and I sat comfortably in the blue Lazy Boy chair beside her.

"Do you have a boyfriend?"

"No, Mom."

"Why not?"

"Because I don't need a boyfriend. I'm happy without one."

She smiled widely and gave me the thumbs up. "Smart girl!" she said.

I felt myself smiling inside, since this sort of conversation used to annoy me. My mother never lost an opportunity to ask me whether I was in a relationship before and after she got dementia. Now, I thought it was funny because it no longer bothered me. In fact, I saw it as a cute exchange we had together, and I felt closer to her now. I didn't realize it until later that I was accepting my mother instead of judging her.

We talked a bit more. She blew me kisses and I blew them back, another cute thing we'd begun doing. Soon, my mother's eyes closed, and she fell asleep. This was usually my cue to get up and leave, but for some reason, my legs felt heavy and I felt glued to the chair. I sat quietly for a while. I didn't take out my phone to check for messages or rummage in my bag for my lipstick. I sat there and stared at my mother as she slept. And that's when I felt an overwhelming, intoxicating feeling inside. It brought tears to my eyes, and I felt as light as air. Without thinking about what had come over me, I whispered, "I love my mother. Thank you, God. I love my mother." I knew that the feeling I'd wished for had arrived. I could now say with conviction, "I love my mother. I really, really love my mother."

A few moments later, I got up out of my chair, blew my mother a few kisses and whispered, "I love you."

It was the last time I saw my mother alive.

From the moment I arrived in Florida and witnessed the unfolding of my mother's last years, I felt an anxiety each night when I went to sleep. It was beside me when I awoke each morning, and it followed me each day like a shadow. *How would my mother's life end?* I'd think about my father's sudden death in 2012, where I didn't have the chance to say goodbye. My mother was ninety and a half years old. Her time on this earth was limited.

As I played out the different scenarios in my mind, I was terrified of what the future would bring. I feared her health would worsen, and she'd lose a limb to diabetes. I worried that her dementia would advance, and she'd forget her life, who she was, and who I was. It didn't help that I was also squeamish of hospitals and being surrounded by illness.

I hoped my mother would pass peacefully in her sleep one night, but that as long as her quality of life was good, it wouldn't happen for many years. I've known people who had a reasonable quality of life well into their nineties and even passed one hundred years old. But my anxiety worsened when I saw indications that her dementia was worsening. I didn't know how to prepare myself for the day my mother wouldn't recognize me or the possibility that she could become combative and hostile toward me. I dismissed these thoughts quickly.

As time passed, my mother developed other health challenges we didn't expect, like the blood clot in her lung. "My mother dodged another bullet," I'd say. It was God's will. My mother survived so many things in her life, both in circumstances and in health, that I was beginning to think she'd live forever. But I knew that wasn't possible. I'd pray that she wouldn't lose a limb or suffer in any way. I stayed close to home even when things were good. I turned down invitations to weddings out-of-town so I wouldn't be away, just in case. I slept with my phone close by and hoped for its silence as I slept.

When my mother's leg became painful and swollen, it was determined she had cellulitis, an infection of the skin. She was susceptible to outbreaks of cellulitis after the lymph nodes under her arm were removed during surgery for breast cancer in her early seventies. Each time she had a flareup, she had to be hospitalized and given intravenous antibiotics. This time, she was admitted to the hospital not only for treatment of the cellulitis, but to have surgery to improve the circulation in her leg. During the surgery, however, the surgeon elected to not proceed because there were indications she needed more extensive surgery that he felt would put her life in danger. She'd have to live with her condition and lose some of her mobility.

Once she was released from the hospital, she was on bedrest for the next two weeks. She had all meals in bed and wasn't permitted to use the bathroom, either. Elisa and her two daughters, Lois and Tanisha, took turns to ensure my mother wasn't left alone for a moment. Soon, my mother was back on her feet and doing okay.

A week later, she had her scheduled follow-up appointment with her doctor on Friday morning at 10:00 a.m. Elisa volunteered to take my mother to the doctor so that I could keep my scheduled appointments, which included lunch with a friend. I was grateful and accepted Elisa's offer. I then planned to visit my mother to discuss her doctor's visit after my lunch.

Being the control freak that I am, I wondered whether I should be at that doctor's visit. I always took copious notes and asked the doctor questions others don't think to ask. But Elisa assured me she would be on top of it and write down all instructions.

Friday morning arrived, and I rose early as usual to walk my dogs and feed them their breakfast. As I was tying my sneakers, I contemplated whether I should cancel my appointments and meet my mother at the doctor's office. I thought again about doing this as I walked the dogs. I was preoccupied with a potpourri of thoughts. *You should be there. No one listens as intently as you do. You can ask the doctor questions. Your mother would love for you to be there. Go. You should go.* Then, I'd hear the chorus of thoughts for keeping things as they were. *Don't be so controlling and anxious. Your mother is going to be fine. You say you want to delegate more, so delegate. Elisa is more than capable of handling this.* It went back and forth a few times.

Then, suddenly, my puppy, Priscilla, vomited on the street four times. Anyone who knows me knows that if my dogs are sick, plans are canceled without a question. When I returned home, I was in the process of texting my girlfriend, Linda, to cancel our lunch. As I clicked the key, I heard a strong voice in my head say, "Wait ten minutes. Priscilla will be fine." So, I erased the text, and sure enough, Priscilla brought me a toy. Her eyes were bright, and she seemed fine. I took this as a sign and decided to keep plans as they were. I kept my early phone meeting and headed out to meet my friend at noon.

"I need to keep my phone out," I said apologetically to Linda. I explained that my mother had a 10:00 a.m. follow-up visit at the doctor and needed to keep my phone close in case Elisa or the doctor needed to speak with me. I suspected that since it was noon everything went well and that my mother was headed back to the facility for lunch.

As Linda and I chatted, I began to feel ill. I felt a migraine coming on, and my stomach started churning. I excused myself and went to the ladies' room where I became quite sick. I didn't return to the table for about fifteen minutes. When I returned, I told Linda I wasn't well. I drank some water, breathed a bit, and felt a little better.

"I'm probably going to head home and see my mother tomorrow," I told Linda as we stood to go. After saying goodbye to Linda, I decided to make a quick visit to the facility to check on my mother since it was right down the road.

When I arrived at the facility, I checked her room and the dining room, but I couldn't find my mother. I asked a staff member who told me she was at a doctor's appointment. "That was at 10:00 a.m.," I told her. She shook her head and replied, "No, the appointment was at 1:00."

I was confused as to how I was convinced her appointment was at 10:00. I shrugged it off and got back in my car. *I'm going to go home and get into bed. Tomorrow's another day.*

When I got in the car, I discovered a voice message from Elisa. She was speaking quickly and frantically. "Your mother wasn't breathing well at the doctor's office. She seemed out of sorts and felt ill. The doctor had us take her down the street to the emergency room. We're at the hospital."

I drove quickly. My heart was pounding as I headed to the hospital that was five minutes away. Just before I made the turn onto the street that leads straight to the emergency room, my sister called me. She was crying. I could hardly make out what she was saying until her crying escalated and she said it again. "Mommy died."

"Please let me in!"

Once I got to the ER and located the room where my mother was, I found myself in front of a closed curtain. I was scared and shaking. I heard movement and asked to be let in.

"Just a moment," the nurse replied.

I was impatient and anxious, so I yelled out. "Please let me in!"

The nurse peeked outside. "Are you a relative?" she asked.

"I'm her daughter."

Susan was very compassionate. She told me how sorry she was and proceeded to tell me what had happened. Apparently, Elisa had to call for help because my mother couldn't breathe, and she couldn't move her out of the car. Three hospital staff came out quickly and got my mother out of the car. They rushed her into the ER and had to take measures to revive her, as her breathing had stopped. The doctor called ahead and told them about the "Do Not Resuscitate Order," so they stopped. She said my mother probably wouldn't have been saved even without the order, because they'd been trying for some time before the doctor intervened.

It felt surreal. Nothing seemed real or tangible. Was I was living this or not?

I sat down beside my mother and took her still-warm hand. I broke into tears and called out to her, "Mommy, Mommy, Mommy." I told her I loved her and that she'll be fine. But I couldn't help noticing the look on her face. It looked as if she'd seen a monster coming to kill her. I slightly squeezed her hand hoping she would squeeze me back. I hoped that there had been a mistake, and she'd be fine. But she just laid there lifeless. Even in death, she didn't look peaceful. Her life was hardly a breeze. I had so much respect for her in that moment. I realized how brave and courageous she really was.

The nurse handed me a small box of orange juice. I held it in my hands, remembering how, not too long ago, I'd helped my mother drink from a tiny straw when we were in a room much like this one during one of her medical scares. It was a simple gesture I wished I could do for her now. I wished I could tell her that she dodged another bullet and that she'd be fine. I ached at the thought that it was all over. Once again, I didn't have the opportunity to say goodbye. I wondered if my illness in the restaurant had happened simultaneously with my mother's death. Everything felt strange and yet connected.

My sister and her husband arrived. I gave them their privacy and stood outside the curtain for a while. Even for those few minutes, it was hard to leave my mother.

Susan came over to me and smiled. "I remember you. I was one of the nurses here when your mother came in a few months ago. I remember her well."

"Oh yes." I said, but it was just to be courteous. Susan didn't look familiar. But I was glad she was here now. She helped me feel comforted, and I appreciated her attention.

"I can see the resemblance," she said. "Especially in the eyes. You and your mother. You're so alike."

That's when tears of joy began to fall. This was something I never expected to happen in my lifetime. What I once resisted, I now welcomed with an open heart. I took joy in hearing the similarities between me and my mother.

Per her wishes, my mother was cremated. Two weeks after a service we held to honor her, I was looking through hundreds of pictures of my life. Each time I came across my mother, I'd study it hoping to find the resemblance and thrilled when I did. I can also say that I never expected to be as devastated by losing her as I have been. It's been heart wrenching, and I still break down in tears at the most unexpected times.

Today, I can authentically declare the love for my mother. Using the steps within this book got me to where I am today: proud to be my mother's daughter and proud to call Livia Rosenberg my mother.

THE FINAL STEP: MAKE THE CHOICE TO FORGIVE. IT'S A CHOICE.

At some point, after taking the recommended steps and opening your heart to become willing to forgive, you must make the choice to jump in.

I was overjoyed to have reached the place of peace in my heart for my mother before she left the physical world. That was a true gift. It's possible and effective to forgive others after death, too, but there's something extra special about forgiving someone that's still here, especially if you're in each other's lives.

Once you make the choice to forgive, all the benefits will present themselves. For me, it's the good memories I have that are devoid of resentment. I also think about all the good things my mother did do for me, specifically giving me life and all the other things that supported me in becoming the woman I am today. She did get a lot of things right. I choose to highlight these positive thoughts today and allow the negative or bad thoughts to take care of themselves.

Regardless of my judgments about my mother as a mother, she was a woman with a big heart and a broken heart. She suffered much trauma in her life. I hope she'll experience much healing in her soul. I also hope that she's happy wherever she is. I miss her every day.

It's now up to you to make a choice. What do you want to do? If you want to live a happy life filled with joy and opportunity, I hope you will forgive your mother. I hope you'll forgive as many people as you're willing, whether they remain in your life or not.

Remember. Forgiveness is for you.

Live well and don't stop.

EPILOGUE

Two weeks before the deadline for my manuscript, I got very sick and couldn't write for days.

There aren't words to describe the strange feelings coming up for me during this time, other than to say the feelings weren't mine. At least, *who I am* today.

I slept constantly and was barely able to care for my two dogs. I reached out to my sister to bring me the only foods I could stomach, plain bagels and boiled potatoes. After those made me feel worse, I requested chicken broth and Jell-O. Even then, I couldn't shake the migraine headache despite the medication I was taking regularly. Vomiting, something I usually dreaded, was now a welcoming relief. There were moments when I thought I wouldn't recover. There were scarier moments when I didn't want to.

After waking up from a long stretch of sleep, I'd look around my home as if it wasn't mine. I didn't feel gratitude for the things around me as I normally did. I felt angry and hateful. I wondered whether something was seriously wrong with me. I had to use every ounce of strength and every energy technique I knew to pull myself out of bed and *shake it off.* Eventually, the angry, hateful feelings subsided, and I'd feel normal again. But then they would return. After spending time in contemplation, I realized what was going on.

This book wasn't an easy one for me to write. I chose to do it for my mother and my family so that we can heal. I wrote it for you, my dear reader, so that you may experience the joy of forgiveness. But I must admit that as my words filled the page, I found myself taking an unwanted trip back to the days I was writing about, not literally of course, but very close to it. I was taking on the essence and personality of who I was at the time, while I was composing the words about my experiences onto paper.

For instance, one day, after spending the morning writing, I sat comfortably in my den with my two fur babies at either side watching a show about house renovations, which I thoroughly enjoy. Unexpectedly, I got a strong craving for a vodka martini with big green olives, the ones stuffed with pimentos.

What? A martini? I barely even drink wine these days. The feeling was so strong, I even imagined getting dressed to go to the store to buy the necessary ingredients. Now, had I done just that and enjoyed a martini, it would hardly be the end of the world, but it wasn't me! When the craving returned several more times over the next week, I finally got the shopping part out of the way.

I have yet to enjoy the martini. I did realize, though, that as I was writing about the days when I craved them, I was emotionally returning to that time. Back then, I was somewhat of a lush when it came to martinis. Today, I could reason with myself that having a martini had consequences. I wouldn't feel good afterwards, since I'm allergic to brewer's yeast and don't do well with fermented alcohol.

But having a martini wasn't the only side effect of my writing. I also realized that my emotional eating had picked up quite a bit, too. I was ordering pizza and Chinese food every week and decided I'd never diet again. I was gaining weight, and I didn't care. I was consuming all the pleasure I could and finally enjoying it without judgment or guilt. It was a fun party while it lasted.

As I write this now, having recovered from the headache, nausea, and weird out-of-body experiences, I'm reminded of Eckhart Tolle's book, *The Power of Now*. In it, he struggles with living one more day with *himself!* I could relate! I had a strong desire to bang my head against the wall, as if I was fighting to get something out of me or to get away from a part of myself, which consumed me for a time. I was experiencing an intense degree of self-loathing. I was able to finally convince myself to breathe and relax. The feeling passed, and I hope I never experience it again. I must admit, though, I did get a doozy of an epiphany out of all this that increased my forgiveness for my mother, and especially for me!

I'm convinced that I went back in time to my earlier days while I was reliving them on paper. The thoughts I was thinking and the feelings I was having were exactly how I felt in the past. Because I was emotionally tuning out back then, I didn't feel the intensity of what plagued me. This time, I got a full dose being fully sober. I realize that my struggle was much bigger than I thought. I now see my past *bad choices* were influenced by a force so compelling it couldn't be reasoned with or tamed. I was clearly traumatized in those days and had a poor self-image. I've summed it up into a phrase that says it all: *Survival is a full-time job.*

When we're traumatized, we're too busy staying afloat to pay attention to how we're swimming. Breathing is all that matters. I believe we do what we do, including all the sabotage, because it's our way of surviving our hell. Surviving is about swimming to the top of the water to catch our breath. Thriving is about climbing out of the water and standing on dry land. It comes with deep healing and commitment and involves a journey that we must all take on our own.

I believe my sick time was a test to see if I'd fight to forgive that part of me I still blamed for making such bad decisions. Even though I live an extraordinary life today, she wasn't fully welcome to join me, until now. Even though I don't like this intruder, she helped me get to where I am today. I must love and welcome her as part of my journey. I must forgive her, too. I am happier and more grateful for having birthed this book, regardless of what I needed to go through to make it happen.

I hope that you keep forgiving yourself for all the things you regret, or wish hadn't happened. Self-forgiveness is the biggest step we can take on our behalf. The hope is that we do it sooner rather than later so we can start enjoying and claiming the life we all deserve: a happy, joyous one where we love ourselves and dance with others in harmony.

I wish this for you now and always.

NOTES

A Note to the Reader:

1. Schucman, H. (2007). *A Course in Miracles.* The Foundation for Inner Peace.

Chapter 3:

2. Child Neglect. (2020, March 20) In *Wikipedia.* Retrieved from https://en.wikipedia.org/wiki/Child neglect.

Chapter 7:

3. Schucman, H. (2007). *A Course in Miracles.* The Foundation for Inner Peace.

Chapter 8:

1. Millie Perkins. *The Diary of Anne Frank.* Directed by George Stevens. Beverly Hills, CA: Twentieth Century Fox, 1959.
2. Liam Neeson, Ben Kingsley. *Schindler's List.* Directed by Steven Spielberg. Universal City, CA: Universal Pictures, 2004.
3. Adrien Brody. *The Pianist.* Directed by Roman Polanski. Universal City, CA: Universal Studios, 2003.
4. Kate Winslet, Ralph Fiennes. *The Reader.* Directed by Stephen Daldry. Santa Monica, CA: Weinstein Co., 2009.
5. Faye Dunaway. *Mommie Dearest.* Directed by Frank Perry. Los Angeles, CA: Paramount Pictures Corporation, 1981.

Chapter 12:

6. Paul, M. & Chopich, E. (1990). *Healing Your Aloneness – Finding Love and Wholeness Through Your Inner Child.* HarperCollins Publishers.

Epilogue:

7. Tolle, E. (2010). *The Power of Now.* New World Library.

ADDITIONAL RESOURCES

Here are some resources I highly recommend that have supported me on my journey toward forgiveness.

1. Margaret Paul and Erika Chopich, *Healing Your Aloneness – Finding Love and Wholeness Through Your Inner Child*, HarperCollins Publishers, 1990.

2. David Hawkins, *Dealing with the CrazyMakers in Your Life: Setting Boundaries on Unhealthy Relationships*, Harvest House Publishers, 2007.

3. Debbie Ford, *The Secret of the Shadow – The Power of Owning Your Whole Story*, HarperCollins Publishers, 2003.

4. Patrick J. Carnes, Ph.D., *The Betrayal Bond – Breaking Free of Exploitive Relationships*, Health Communications, Inc., 1997, 2019.

ABOUT THE AUTHOR

Eve Rosenberg is an Integrative Life Coach and the author of *Your Happy Life Realized, How to Stop Putting Others First and Yourself Last Now!* and *Be Selfish, Eat Well, Serve Many*. Eve compassionately supports others to step into their lives with both feet and create relationships that are joyful and intimate with themselves and others.

Born to Holocaust survivors to save their unhappy marriage, Eve has experienced trauma and drama in her life. As an avid People Pleaser for decades, she understands how this destructive behavior has wreaked havoc in her relationships. Chasing love through the opinions and accolades of others, Eve knows what it's like to feel lonely, unworthy, and lost. She also knows with certainty that despite what we've lived through, there is correction and renewal available whenever we're ready to claim it.

"Everything that has taken me to today has been for a reason. Therefore, I love yesterday, embrace today, and cherish tomorrow."

Along with being impeccably trained as a Master Integrative Coach by the late Debbie Ford and the Ford Institute for Transformational Training, Eve holds a Bachelor of Arts degree in sociology/psychology, a certification as a Holistic Health and Wellness Counselor, and has a vast employment history in corporate America. She lives in sunny Florida with her two dogs, Tabitha and Priscilla.

Made in the USA
Monee, IL
11 February 2021